Candidate Name	Centre Number	Candidate Number

OCR
RECOGNISING ACHIEVEMENT

OXFORD CAMBRIDGE AND RSA EXAMINATIONS

General Certificate of Secondary Education

INFORMATION AND COMMUNICATION TECHNOLOGY

2359/02

PAPER 3 (HIGHER TIER)

Friday **20 JANUARY 2006** Afternoon 1 hour 15 minutes

Candidates answer on the question paper.
No additional materials are required.

CW01677984

TIME 1 hour 15 minutes

INSTRUCTIONS TO CANDIDATES

Write your name, Centre number and candidate number in the spaces at the top of this page.

Answer **all** the questions.

Write your answers, in blue or black ink, in the spaces on the question paper.

INFORMATION FOR CANDIDATES

The number of marks is given in brackets [ ] at the end of each question or part question.

No marks will be awarded for using brand names of software packages or hardware.

The total number of marks for this paper is **60**.

FOR EXAMINER'S USE ONLY		
Question Number	Maximum Marks	Marks Awarded
1	4	
2	6	
3	7	
4	3	
5	6	
6	4	
7	14	
8	4	
9	6	
10	6	
TOTAL	60	

This question paper consists of 10 printed pages and 2 blank pages.

SP (SC) S90036/4

[Turn over

Milo C.

For Examiner Use

Answer **all** questions.

1 A school has an intranet for the staff and students to use. Some of the files stored on the intranet are confidential.

(a) Give **two** reasons why a school may have an intranet. internet contained on the network.

Reason 1 ~~To keep information secure from any outside user~~ As long as the server is up - Info is always there.

Reason 2 So correct information can be found by the pupils [2]

Staff and students also have access to the Internet.

(b) Give **two** reasons why a school might also need access to the Internet.

Reason 1 Allow research on a wider scale.

Reason 2 Communicate ~~[illegible]~~ to others outside the school. [2]

For Examiner's Use

2 A local authority is planning to send a booklet to disabled people in the area. It will give details about the services the authority offers.

(a) Describe **two** benefits to some disabled people of receiving this information as a multi-media presentation on a CD instead of a booklet.

Benefit 1 Allow ~~deaf~~ blind people to hear the parts of the presentation which have audio.

Benefit 2 Allow deaf people to ~~tex~~ read text in places where there is ~~~~ audio.

[4]

(b) Give **two** disadvantages for some disabled people of receiving the information on a CD.

Disadvantage 1 May not have the equipment to play the CD.

Disadvantage 2 The person may also be epileptic

[2]

For Examiner's Use

3 Tacita Jones works in a garage. She wants to invite all of the customers to test drive a new car. She has prepared this document which is now ready to be mail-merged.

ORC Cars
Motor Lane
Greenhampton
Middleshire
GT6 8JK

12 January 2006

<<Title>> <<FirstName>> <<LastName>>
<<Address1>>
<<Address2>>
<<City>>

Dear **<<Title>> <<LastName>>**

We are pleased to give **<<Title>> <<FirstName>> <<LastName>>** the opportunity to test drive, for one week, our latest Zebra X34 luxury saloon car. To arrange a mutually convenient time, please contact Mr Harry Sousa on 01923 746753 during the next two weeks.

Yours sincerely

T Jones
Sales and Customer Service Manager

(a) Describe the steps she has taken to prepare this document and the further steps needed to produce the individual invitations ready to be sent to different customers.

- Created a Database. (customer details)
- wrote a letter
- Insert merge fields
- Complete merge / choose customers.
- Print out specific customers that are needed.

[5]

For Examiner's Use

(b) Give **two** advantages to the garage of using mail-merge to send out information to its customers rather than typing each letter individually.

Advantage 1 Saves time because you only have to write the letter

Advantage 2 Cuts out ~~mistakes~~ human error. [2]

4 The first stage in the creation of a new ICT system is to investigate the existing system.

Fill in the table below stating which investigation method would be used in the given circumstances.

When appropriate	Investigation method
When a large number of people need to be consulted	Qestionnaire
To confirm what **actually** happens in the present system	~~Intervi~~ Observation
When a few key personnel need to be consulted	Interview.

[3]

5 A Local Area Network (LAN) has a server and three workstations. One possible topology for this network is shown in Fig.1.
Draw, name and label **two** other possible topologies.

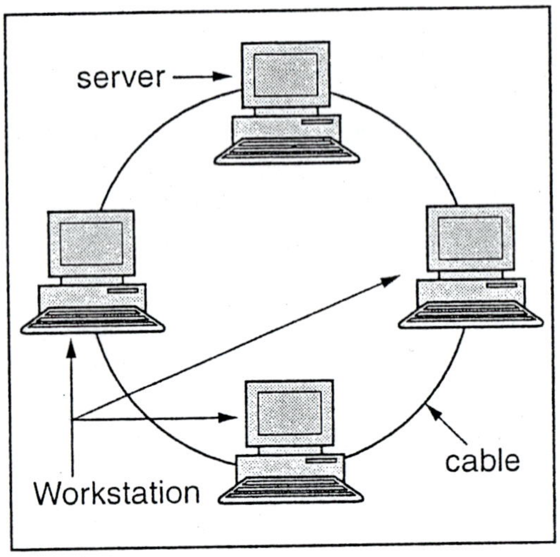

Name: **Ring**

Fig. 1

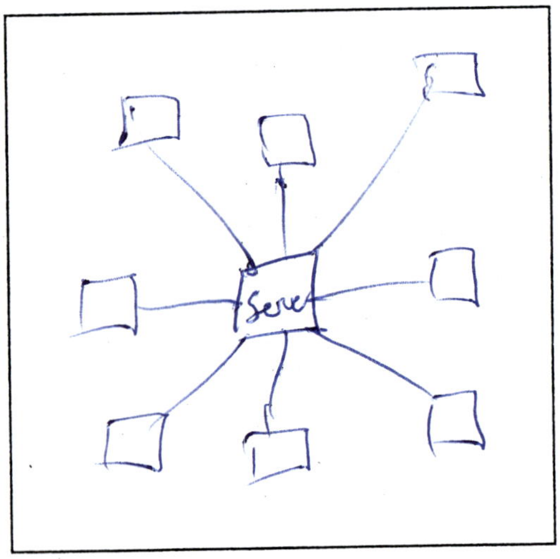

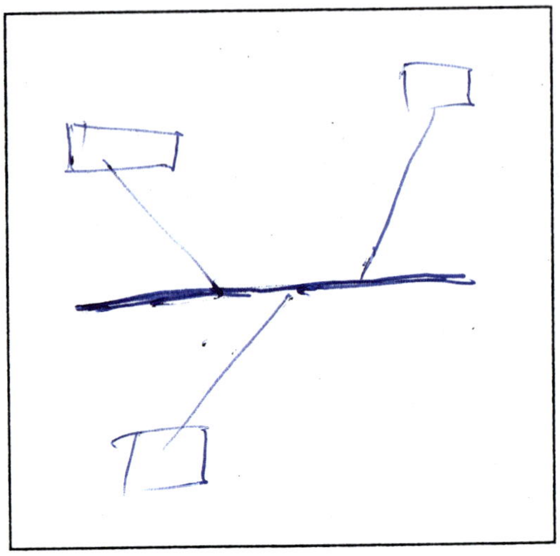

Name: ....Star.......... Name: ....Bus.......... [6]

For Examiner's Use

6 The use of mobile phones to take and send digital pictures is now common.

(a) Give **two** benefits of taking and sending pictures using a mobile phone.

Benefit 1 Portable mobile phones

Benefit 2 Easily send to whichever person you want.

[2]

(b) Give **two** problems that may arise from using a mobile phone to take pictures.

Problem 1 The camera may not be of a high quality.

Problem 2 The phone ~~do~~ has a small memory capacity

[2]

For Examiner's Use

7 A dentist's surgery needs to collect information about new patients. Each new patient would be asked to give their name, address, date of birth, and details about their last visit.

(a) In the box below design a screen input form that will allow this information to be entered as accurately as possible.

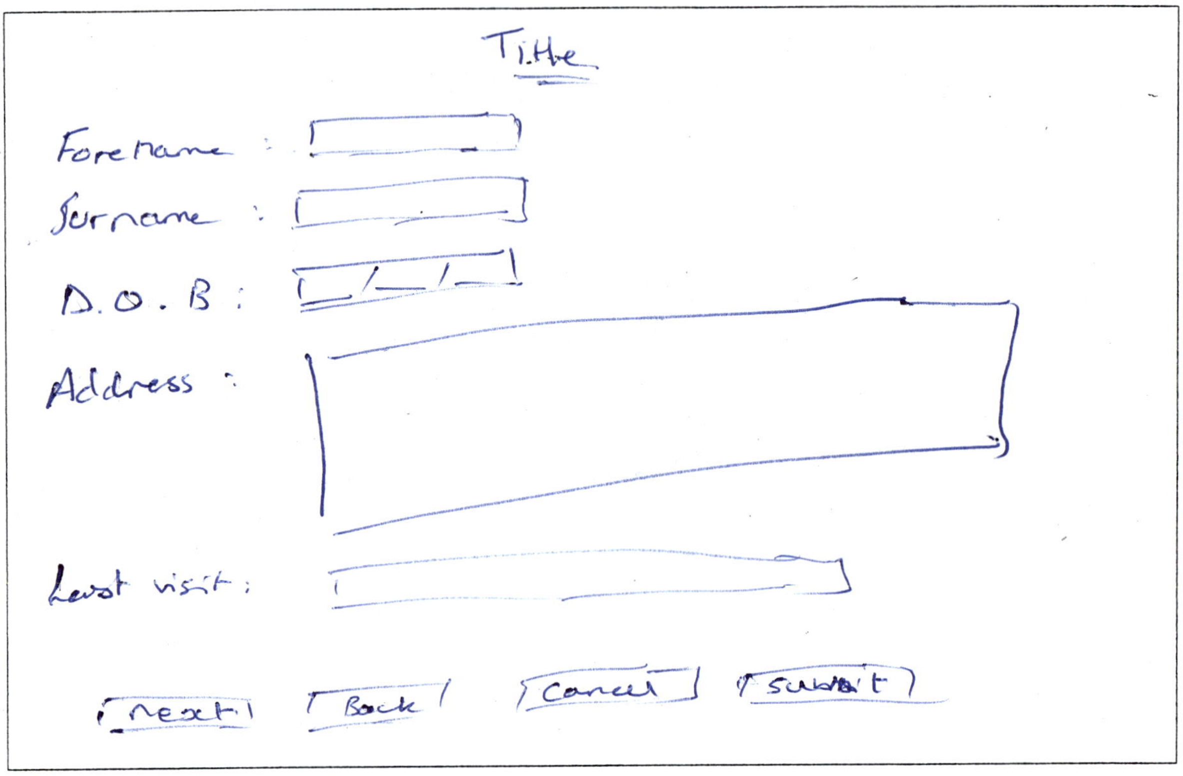

[5]

(b) State **three** different principles of the Data Protection Act which the dentist would need to comply with. Explain why each is important.

Principle 1 .... Accurate + up2date. ....

This is important because .... In case of emergencies ....

....

....

....[3]

Principle 2 .... Don't keep info for longer than needed ....

This is important because .... Don't end up in wrong ....

.... hands. ....

....

....[3]

For Examiner's Use

Principle 3 ....needs authorisation.......................................

This is important because ....

....

....

....[3]

8 Bar codes contain check digits.

(a) State the purpose of a check digit.

....Validate the product..[1]

(b) Explain how check digits are used in bar codes.

.... - extra digit for ↓...

.... - mathmatical equation...

....

....

....

....[3]

9 An organisation has decided to replace its old manual administration system with a computerised system.

Explain **three** tasks that need to be carried out during the design of the new system.

Task 1 ....Research existing system.......................................

....

....

....

Task 2 ....Analyse findings...

....

....

....

Task 3 ....design...

....

.... [6]

For Examiner Use

10 *'The Internet has created more problems than benefits for schools.'*
Discuss this statement.

- plageism
- pornography
- distractions
- incorrect dat

} bad.

- wider range of reaserch
- multimedia

} good.

[6]

Candidate Name	Centre Number	Candidate Number

OCR RECOGNISING ACHIEVEMENT

OXFORD CAMBRIDGE AND RSA EXAMINATIONS
General Certificate of Secondary Education

INFORMATION AND COMMUNICATION TECHNOLOGY

2359/02

PAPER 3 (HIGHER TIER)

Tuesday **7 JUNE 2005** Morning 1 hour 15 minutes

Candidates answer on the question paper.
No additional materials are required.

TIME 1 hour 15 minutes

INSTRUCTIONS TO CANDIDATES

Write your name, Centre number and candidate number in the spaces at the top of this page.

Answer **all** the questions.

Write your answers, in blue or black ink, in the spaces on the question paper.

INFORMATION FOR CANDIDATES

The number of marks is given in brackets [ ] at the end of each question or part question.

No marks will be awarded for using brand names of software packages or hardware.

The total number of marks for this paper is **60**.

FOR EXAMINER'S USE	
1	
2	
3	
4	
5	
6	
7	
8	
9	
10	
11	
12	
13	
TOTAL	

This question paper consists of 9 printed pages and 3 blank pages.

For Examiner's Use

Answer **all** questions.

1 State **three** different methods a systems analyst might use to collect information about a system that the systems analyst is investigating.

Method 1 Questionnaire

Method 2 Interview

Method 3 Observation [3]

2 A company uses batch processing to produce wage slips for its employees.

Give **two** reasons why 'real-time processing' is **not** used for this task. ← Process carried out straight away.

Reason 1 Same thing over again so it is easier to do it all in one.

Reason 2 It doesn't need to carry out real time processing. [2]

3 Before creating a database the file structure has to be designed.

Give **two** items that need to be included in the design of the file structure.

Item 1 field names.

Item 2 field size [2]

For Examiner's Use

4 Most supermarkets have Point-of-Sale (POS) terminals which use bar code readers to input data. These produce itemised bills for customers.

(a) Give **two** advantages to the customer of receiving an itemised bill.

Advantage 1 See how much each item has cost.

Advantage 2 Proof of purchase

[2]

(b) Give **two** advantages to the supermarket of giving the customer an itemised bill.

Advantage 1 Stock control

Advantage 2 proof of selling.

[2]

(c) Explain how an automatic stock control system linked to the POS terminals would work.

- Bar code scanned
- Data fed into computer system.
- Number of goods sold taken away from stock
- When stock goes below a certain level, new stock is ordered.

[5]

For Examiner's Use

5 The final stage in the systems life cycle process is evaluation. Identifying the good and bad points of the final system is one part of this evaluation stage.

Describe **two** other processes undertaken during the evaluation stage.

Process 1 Any other changes that could be made.

....

....

....

Process 2 Analyse user's comments.

....

....

....[4]

6 A Training Officer is to give a multi-media presentation. She has a laptop computer with a fast processor, graphics card and the appropriate software already installed.

Describe the use of **two** extra items of hardware she might use for developing and displaying the presentation.

Item 1 Projector

....

....

....

....

Item 2 digital camera

....

....

....

....[4]

For Examiner's Use

7 An aid organisation wishes to keep in touch with its representatives throughout the world. As each of its representatives already has access to a computer they have decided to investigate the use of video conferencing.

(a) State **two** additional items of hardware the representatives would need for video conferencing.

Item 1 Web camera

Item 2 Moden [2]

(b) **(i)** Give **two** advantages to the organisation of using video conferencing in this situation.

Advantage 1 reduce travel costs.

Advantage 2 talk to many people at the same time around the world. [2]

(ii) Give **two** disadvantages to the aid worker of using video conferencing in this situation.

Disadvantage 1 More equipment required.

Disadvantage 2 Poor quality connection. [2]

8 Three methods of changing from an old system to a new one are:

- Direct changeover (Big Bang)
- Phased implementation
- Parallel running

Give **one** advantage of using each of these methods.

Direct changeover (Big Bang) Faster way of changover.

Phased implementation Each section can be tested before you go to the next stage.

Parallel running If the new system doesn't work very well you can go back to the old one. [3]

[Turn over

For Examiner's Use

9 Validation and verification are two ways of checking data entered into a computer.

Describe, using an example for each, what these two terms mean.

Validation Checking it is the correct format for entry → Range check.

Verification Checking if data is accurate. (two people) twin entry, dual entry. (typed twice)

[6]

For Examiner's Use

10 A market gardener uses a computer-controlled system to keep the humidity in a large greenhouse suitable for growing plants. The system contains these components:

- a computer (3)
- analogue to digital converters (ADC's) (2)
- humidity sensors (1)
- actuators (4)
- humidifiers (devices which spray water into the atmosphere to keep the air humid) (5)
- motors for the windows (5)

Describe how these components form a control-feedback loop in this closed system.

....

....

....

....

....

....

....

....

....

....

....

....[6]

[Turn over

For Examiner's Use

11 Beth works on a computer in a government department. She needs to archive and backup her data.

Describe the differences between the terms archive and backup and explain why Beth needs to do both.

Archive → removed from system but is kept for a certain period of time.
Backup → Make a copy of data in the system

Joe was here

....[5]

12 A large company is to install a star network.

Discuss the advantages and disadvantages of a star network compared to other network topologies.

- Very fast but
- Expensive
- Server goes down, everything goes down
- Levels of access.
- one cable / computer goes down none other are effected
- easy to add nodes
- apply security
- needs a systems administrator

....[5]

For Examiner's Use

13 'Computer Assisted Learning will do away with the need for Universities.'

Discuss this statement.

- Live where ever you live.

...[5]

BLANK PAGE

CGP	Practice Exam Paper GCSE ICT

General Certificate of Secondary Education

GCSE
Information and Communication Technology (ICT)

Centre name	Altrincham Grammar for boys.				
Centre number	3	3	6	1	1
Candidate number		1	0	7	9

Exam 1 Paper A
Higher Tier

Surname	LADU
Other names	EMMANUEL
Candidate signature	

Time allowed: 1 hour 30 minutes

Instructions to candidates
- Write your name and other details in the spaces provided above.
- Answer **all** questions in the spaces provided.
- Do all rough work on the paper.

Information for candidates
- The marks available are given in brackets at the end of each question or part-question.
- Marks will not be deducted for incorrect answers.
- In calculations show clearly how you work out your answers.
- There are 13 questions in this paper. There is one blank page.

Advice to candidates
- Work steadily through the paper.
- Don't spend too long on one question.
- If you have time at the end, go back and check your answers.

For examiner's use

Q	Attempt Nº			Q	Attempt Nº		
	1	2	3		1	2	3
1				8			
2				9			
3				10			
4				11			
5				12			
6				13			
7							
				Total 80			

Leave blank

1 Pushem High School has three computer rooms. The computers are connected together in a local area network (LAN). The LAN uses a ring configuration.

(a) Give two differences between a local area network and a wide area network.

Difference 1 WAN's need modem's to connect to the server.

Difference 2 WAN's are used by teleworkers who work in different countries

(2 marks)

(b) (i) Explain how a ring configuration differs from a line configuration.

Ring configuration means that all the data flows around all the equiptment in one direction only.

(2 marks)

(ii) Give one benefit and one drawback of a ring configuration.

Benefit Fast as data flows in only one direction.

Drawback Lots of users make the system slower.

(2 marks)

(c) Pupils who use the school's computer network are given usernames and passwords.

Give one reason why pupils should change their password frequently.

To prevent other students from managing to hack into other accounts.

(1 mark)

2 Barker's Bank issues all of its customers with a bank card. The card can be used to withdraw cash from ATMs and be used to make EFTPOS purchases in shops.

Leave blank

(a) What do the initials ATM stand for?

Automatic Telling Machine

(1 mark)

(b) Describe what happens when a customer obtains cash from an ATM.

When a customer obtains cash from an ATM they put their card in the ATM and the user enters their pin. A magnetic reader in the ATM reads the card and accepts the pin. The user can now select how much they would like to take out.

(3 marks)

(c) What does EFTPOS stand for?

Electronic Funds Transfer at the Point Of Sale

(2 marks)

(d) Banks take a number of measures to try to prevent the fraudulent use of bank cards.

Explain one method that a bank can use to help prevent card fraud.

The bank issues the user withe security methods such as verification Signatures and pin numbers.

(2 marks)

3 An estate agent stores details of properties for sale in a manual filing system. The manager is thinking of introducing a computerised system.

Give two ways that the estate agent might benefit from storing data on a computer system.

Benefit 1 Decreases the risk of human error.

Benefit 2 More details can be stored and ~~easy~~ made easier to access.

(2 marks)

4 Ivor Flashcar has air-conditioning in his new car. When the temperature inside the car rises above a preset temperature the air-conditioner cools the car down. When the temperature falls below the preset level, the air-conditioner heats the car.

(a) Identify one sensor that the air-conditioning system might use.

heat / thermistor.

(1 mark)

(b) Describe how the air-conditioning system would work if Ivor wanted the temperature inside the car to be 21 degrees Celsius.

When the temperature gets above 21 degrees the heat sensor senses this and turns on the air conditioning. As the temp falls below 21° then the heater comes on to heat the car.

(4 marks)

Leave blank

Leave blank

5 Jane has collected the following information for a History project:

King	Start of Reign	End of Reign
Richard II	1377	1399
Henry IV	1399	1413
Henry V	1413	1422
Henry VI	1422	1461

Jane wants to calculate how long each king reigned and then create a graph to display the results.

Explain how Jane could use a spreadsheet and graphing software to do this.

She could create another column which calculated the length of reign. This column and the king column would then be selected and the graph option selected. Jane could then follow the on screen instructions

(4 marks)

6 The following are items of computer hardware found in a weather station:

thermistor, graph plotter, keyboard, pressure sensor, VDU, central processing unit.

(a) Which items are input devices?

thermistor, keyboard, pressure sensor

(b) Which items are output devices?

Graph plotter, VDU

(5 marks)

Le
bla

7 Barry Bison owns a number of butcher's shops in Cumbria.

(a) Bison's Butchers sells its Cumberland sausages on the internet using an online shopping service. Customers pay for their sausages by credit card. The data is kept secure by using data encryption software.

Explain what is meant by 'data encryption'.

Data is ~~encrypted~~ converted using a special code

which can only be encrypted by the ~~new~~ correct encryption software

(2 marks)

(b) Doris Bison collects customer orders from the web site. She also keeps the firm's accounts and looks after the personnel database. She often spends a long time working at her computer.

(i) Identify two possible health risks from working long hours at a computer.

Risk 1 She could get RSI

....

Risk 2 She could develop poor eyesight.

....

(2 marks)

(ii) List two actions that Doris could take to help reduce the health risks of using computers.

Action 1 take ~~~~~ breaks every hour

....

Action 2 work in a well lighted room

....

(2 marks)

8 Sally Screamer is an assistant headteacher at Pushem High School. The school keeps information about its pupils on a database.

(a) Sally wants to design a form to collect personal information about new pupils joining the school. Use the space below to design a suitable data-capture form.

Pushem High School

NAME ______________________

DOB ___ / ___ / ___ (DD/MM/YYYY)

ADDRESS ______________________

____

POST CODE ______________________

Phone no. ______________________

(4 marks)

(b) At the end of the school year, Sally produces a newsletter for parents informing them about the events in the school that year. Sally decides to produce the newsletter using desktop publishing software. Explain how Sally could use her computer to produce the newsletter.

By using the desktop publishing software she is able to design a newsletter that suits the school's needs. She would be able to input photo's through either a scanner, digital camera or the internet. She can change different layout styles including the title, background, font, text and even add borders if she wants to.

(6 marks)

Leave blank

9 Megan wants to collect data on how the temperature of her school science laboratory changes over a four-day period.

(a) Explain how Megan could use data-logging equipment to collect the data.

She could collect the data using sensors and send them to a computer using an ADC to which various outputs ~~like~~ like graphs and reports can be produced.

(3 marks)

(b) Explain how Megan could use computer software to analyse the results of the experiment.

The results can be put into a graph so that each days outcome can be compared and a conclusion drawn up.

(2 marks)

10 Renta-nurse stores details of its nurses and customers on a computerised database. As a result it is required to comply with the Data Protection Act.

(a) Give three restrictions that the Data Protection Act places on organisations such as Renta-nurse.

Restriction 1 Don't keep information longer than needed.

Restriction 2 Data must be accurate + kept up to date if possible.

Restriction 3 Only a specified amount of data should be held + all should be relevant.

(3 marks)

Leave blank

(b) Staff who work at Renta-nurse are required to comply with the Computer Misuse Act and the Copyright, Designs and Patents Act.

Leave blank

Give three restrictions that these laws place on computer users.

Restriction 1 Copying the programme used at work to run it at home.

Restriction 2 Using information from the internet without saying where you got them.

Restriction 3 Using software without a licence.

(3 marks)

11 Phil is setting up a fantasy football league. He will be putting all the data about the players into a database. He has collected the following information about one player:

Wally Thrower, 35 years old, Goalkeeper, Liverham FC

(a) Give a suitable field name for each piece of data.

name:

age:

position:

Club:

(4 marks)

(b) Explain how Phil could use coding to reduce the memory needed to store the database.

instead of using full names for position G could be used instead and age can only be the number to reduce memory.

(2 marks)

12 Punita opens her e-mail account and notices that she has an e-mail from someone she does not know. The e-mail contains an attachment. Punita is worried that the attachment might contain a computer virus.

(a) What is a computer virus?

A programme that can multiply + corrupt files on a compute + can be easily transferred.

(2 marks)

(b) How could Punita check that the attachment is safe to open?

use an antivirus check on the attachment.

(1 mark)

(c) Punita wants to send a photograph of herself to a favourite aunt. She wishes to send it as an e-mail attachment. The photograph was taken using a digital camera.

(i) Describe the steps needed to send the photograph to her aunt.

First thing to do is to log on to her email and create an email. After the message is typed, select the attachment tool then browse for the specific picture. Once uploaded, the email is ready to send.

(3 marks)

(ii) Give two benefits of using e-mail.

Benefit 1 Can be sent directly to reciever

Benefit 2 Much quicker to recieve the message

(2 marks)

(iii) Apart from the possibility of downloading a virus, give two other problems of using e-mail to send and receive messages.

Problem 1 need the internet.

Problem 2 has limits to the number of emails it can hold.

(2 marks)

13 Discuss the social and moral implications of the growth in use of the internet.

Leave blank

....

....

....

....

....

....

....

....

....

....

....

....

....

....

....

....

....

....

....

....

....

....

(6 marks)

BLANK PAGE

Oxford Cambridge and RSA Examinations

General Certificate of Secondary Education

INFORMATION AND COMMUNICATION TECHNOLOGY A **1094**

HIGHER TIER (2357H)

PAPER 1

Specimen Paper 2002

Additional materials:
Candidates answer on the question paper.

TIME 1 hour 15 minutes

Candidate Name	Centre Number	Candidate Number
Emmanuel Ladu.		1079

INSTRUCTIONS TO CANDIDATES

- Write your name in the space above.
- Write your Centre number and Candidate number in the boxes above.
- Answer all the questions.
- Write your answers, in blue or black ink, in the spaces provided on the question paper.
- Read each question carefully and make sure you know what you have to do before starting your answer.

INFORMATION FOR CANDIDATES

- The number of marks is given in brackets [ ] at the end of each question or part question.
- The total number of marks for this paper is 60 .
- You will be awarded marks for the quality of written communication where an answer requires a piece of extended writing.

1 A spreadsheet is used to process data about the number of cars using two car parks over a year.

	A	B	C	D
1	Month	Car park A	Car Park B	Most popular car park
2				
3	January	120	145	=if (B3>C3 , "A" , "B")
4	February	140	135	
5	March	174	201	
6	April	134	120	
7	May	167	130	
8	June	278	290	
9	July	290	315	
10	August	312	289	
11	September	216	290	
12	October	213	278	
13	November	126	178	
14	December	78	98	

(a) Cell D3 shows how the most popular car park for January is calculated. After typing the formula in D3, describe a quick way of putting similar formula into D4 to D14.

The user can highlight the cells from D4 to D14 and then use the fill down tool which will copy the formula into all the cells highlighted.

[2]

(b) Describe how a chart or graph is created to show the use of the car parks over a period of one year.

The user will highlight the cells A1 to A14, B1 to B14 and C1 to C14 then select the chart tool which converts the information to graph. Then add a title then position the graph where you want it.

[2]

(c) **(i)** Give **one** different situation which can be modelled using a computer.

A school trip.

[1]

(ii) Give **two** reasons why a computer model would be useful in this case.

Reason 1 Different costs can be modelled to find the most suitable price.

Reason 2 ~~You can vary the number of pupils and to enable the trip not to be a loss~~

Too time consuming to build a physical model.

[2]

2 **(a)** Give **one** situation where automatic data logging equipment could be used to record data over a long period of time.

~~the~~ weather

[1]

(b) Give **one** reason why automatic data logging equipment should be used to record data over a long period of time?

The data collected is more accurate.

[1]

3 **(a)** What is a computer virus?

a program deliberately written to infect a computer and make copies of itself to corrupt other files which can be passed from computer to computer. [2]

(b) Write down **two** ways in which you could prevent a computer virus affecting your machine.

Way 1 Install an antivirus on your computer to check your computer files.

Way 2 Refrain from going on the internet so others cannot pass the virus.

[2]

4 A school is going to buy a number of laptop computers for pupils to borrow and use at home.

Give **two** problems that this may cause.

Problem 1 The students may use them for improper use e.g. games.

Problem 2 The school may never get the laptops back from the pupils.

[2]

5 A small buggy connected to a computer is placed in a maze. The buggy will travel through the maze and learn the correct path. State **one** sensor which should be attached to the buggy and describe how it would detect an obstacle.

Sensor Light sensor.

Detection when the buggy gets nearer to an obsticle then the light will get darker and darker.

[2]

6 A school secretary uses a computer all day. What **two** pieces of advice would you give to prevent the secretary having medical problems through the use of the computer? Give a reason for each piece of advice.

Advice Make sure that you take regular breaks from the computer

Reason R.S.I -> using the computer too long could give you R.S.I in your hands.

Advice Make sure that you position yourself correctly next to the computer

Reason You could get back problems if you don't sit correctly

[4]

7 A school needs to convert a classroom into an Information Technology room containing 20 computers.

(a) What factors should be taken into account when choosing a suitable classroom?

The room should have a good supply of natural lighting and must be big enough to to hold the 20 computers. Security of the room should also be considered.

[2]

(b) Cost will be one factor in choosing the type of computers to buy. What other factors should be considered?

How much time it would take to train the teachers to use them. They must also ensure that the computer is compatible for all the software that the school uses.

[2]

(c) Give **one** way the introduction of the new computer system will affect the staff and pupils.

The will all have to retrain how to use the new computers.

[1]

8 (a) Give **two** advantages of using an encyclopædia stored on CD-ROM rather than as a book.

Reason 1 The CD-Rom can be transported easily from one computer to another.

Reason 2 The encyclopaedia on CD-Rom will have search facilities making it easy to find information.

[2]

(b) Give **two** reasons why it is preferable to use the book.

Reason 1 May contain more information than the CD-Rom.

Reason 2 You can access the information without needing to use a computer system.

[2]

9 A school is introducing a computerised system for attendance registers. Describe the main stages gone through before the system is operational.

- Analyse new system requirements
- Design new system
- Build new system
- Test new system.
- Documentation for users
- Implement new system
- Maintain new system.
- Evaluate new system.
- Train the teachers.

[4]

10 Describe some of the safety issues which must be considered when setting up a new computer room in a school.

* Trailing cables.

The room must be able to be locked so the computers do not get stolen. Each pupil and member of staff must have password protection to their files to prevent hacking into and seeing their files.

[4]

11 Using an example explain how a computer aided learning system can help pupils learn.

Example: Bite size revision on the internet.

Explanation: The user can either choose to revise particular topics within a subject or to test themselves using the test's provided. If they carry out the tests and get less than a certain percentage, they are recommended to go back and revise the topic again.

[4]

12 A water company uses a sensor to detect the acidity of the water in its reservoirs. Describe what happens to the data from the sensors.

Once the acidity of the water has gone above a certain limit, the sensor sends an analogue message to the main computer, an ADC is used to read the message. The compute now comes up with a message to either inform the company or to send it to the neutralising output using a DAC.

[3]

13 You are producing a school magazine using a desktop-publishing package. Compare alternative methods used to obtain pictures for inclusion in the magazine.

There are many different ways of obtaining images for the magazine. These being; ~~the~~ digital camera, scanner, internet. Copy + pasting from the internet is probably quickest but copywrite laws may have to be observed. Therefore the best method would be getting your own pictures using a digital camera which can be uploaded + is high quality whereas the scanner may be low quality.

[7]

14 Describe how the misuse of computers might give rise to legal and moral problems.

The computer can be used for hacking which is against the law. Through the internet, pornography may be viewed which has moral problems but going into child pornography makes ~~it~~ it into a legal problem. Computers can also be misued by copying copywrited material or communicating to others about terrorist action.

[4]

15 Discuss the advantages and disadvantages of using information technology in shopping.

As we progress in the electronic world, more ~~shopping~~ retail outlets are taking advantage an the one growing in popularity is internet shopping. Advantages such as the saving of time for the shopper or the ease to buy things from the comfort of your own home have made this a huge succesn. Although, there are some drawbacks, unsecure websites may allow some information e.g. Credit card details to be intercepted which inturn could result in the unnecessary purchase of goods. But most of the online-shopping sites have encryption software which mean even if ~~$~~ information is hacked, a speesal key is ~~n~~ needed to view this information. The use of IT in shops has also increased work efficiency by making the worke easier at e.g. Point of Sale stations ~~and~~ to which has made unemployment lower.

[4]

TOTAL MARK 60

14 Description of four points from:
Selling lists of names to other companies e g junk mail.
Hacking to deliberately change data.
Receiving data signals over the air.
Tapping into network cables.
Plagiarism.
Illegal access to personal records.
Storage of personal data.
Fraud
Changing/deleting dat
Pornography
Viruses can be spread
Any other suitable answer. 4

15 Four points from:
Information retrieval system.
Credit cards.
Debit cards.
Security systems in shops.
Automatic money machines.
Running up large bills on credit cards.
Point of Sale machines.
Information systems.
Automated vending machines.
Unemployment.
Automatic doors.
Maximum of two marks on one topic.
Any other suitable answer related to shopping. 4

TOTAL MARK 60

10 Four from:
Positioning of desks/benches
Trailing cables
Electrical safety
Power extensions
Sufficient power points
Any other suitable answer 4

11 Four from:
Questions on screen
Pupils enter answers
Link to next question if correct or link to teaching if incorrect
Guidance through the path
Motivation
Description of a learning system is required. 4

12 Three from:
Data from the sensors is stored in the sensor.
Data from the sensor is transmitted to the computer.
Software can be used to collect data from the sensors.
Software could be used to graph the results.
A word processor can be used to document the results of the test.
Pictures from the data-logging software can be transferred to a word processor.
Publication.
ADC.
Any suitable statements. 3

13 Clipart
Advantages
Freely available
Copyright free when printed
Large source of pre-drawn material
Saves time when creating the document
Disadvantages
Publication could look like many others
Might not have the picture you want
Scanning
Advantages
Can copy any material
Can be used to transfer text into a word processor
Very fast picture acquisition
Disadvantages
Cost of a scanner
Quality of image
Computer memory constraints
User drawn
Advantages
Will be exactly what you want
Disadvantages
Time taken to draw the picture
Need to be talented to produce a good drawing
Any other suitable answers.
Comparison should cover some of the above issues up to a maximum of 7 marks. 7

7 **(a)** Two from:
Size of the room.
Location of the room.
How difficult is it to re-position the staff using the room.
Electricity supply to the room.
Layout of the room.
Can the room be secured?
Any other suitable answer. 2

(b) Two from:
Compatibility of the computers with the other computers in the school.
Is all the required software available for the computers.
How much re-training will be needed if the system is different to what is already in the school?
What maintenance agreements are available on the different computer systems.
Robustness
On-going cost.
Maintenance agreement.
Any other suitable answer. 2

(c) One from:
Training of staff/pupils.
Re-organisation of the timetable.
Upheaval during installation.
Any other suitable answer. 1

8 **(a)** Two from:
Quicker to get the information you want
Search facilities.
Save pictures to other applications
Selectively save text to other applications
Video
Large sound files
Cost of updates
Any other suitable answer 2

(b) Two from:
No computer available
Can be read without needing a computer system
Religious beliefs
Not cost
Any other suitable answer 2

9 The answers should include a description of the following stages:
analysis of the problem
design of the solutions
implementation of the system
evaluation of the system
training
Marks up to a maximum of four. 4

3 **(a)** A piece of software/file which corrupts other software/computer 1
It can be passed from one computer to another computer 1

(b) Two from:
Use a virus scanner.
Software in the computer which checks every disk placed in the drive.
Running a virus checking program which checks every file on the disk.
Do not allow others to place discs in the disk drive.
Write protect floppy discs.
Any other suitable answer. 2

4 Two from:
Pupils may damage the computer (physical/software).
Pupils may lose the computer/stealing.
Pupils may introduce viruses.
Pupils could delete other pupils work.
Pupils could use them for games and not for work.
Pupils may not have a printer to print their work.
Sharing
Training students.
Deleting software.
No handwriting answers.
Any other suitable answer 2

5 One pair from

Switch	contact
Optical	reflection of light
Sound	reflection of sound

Not heat sensor 2

6 Two from:
Lighting
Ergonomic Keyboard
Radiation
Use the correct chair to avoid back problems.
Take regular breaks to avoid eye strain.
Position the keyboard with an arm rest to prevent injury to the wrist.
Any other suitable answer
1 mark for advice. 1 mark for reason. 4

Answers

Where there is only one answer given this is the only answer available.

Where a candidate has to choose a number of answers from a given list there should be no more answers than that asked for in the question. If a candidate gives more answers than asked for then every answer over the specified number cancels out one of the correct answers - if there are any.

No trade names are to given credit unless accompanied by a description of what they do eg 'MS Word' would gain no credit but 'the word processor MS Word' would.

1 **(a)** Highlight cell D3 to D14 1
Replicate (fill, copy) D3 down to D14 1
Any suitable answer

(b) Highlight the areas containing the numbers of cars.
Select the type of chart.
Click on the button/select from a menu to create a graph.
Add title/legend/colour etc (1)
Position the graph on the screen. 2

(c) **(i)** One from:
Flight simulation
Financial modelling
Bridge construction
Must be modelling - not recording
Any other suitable answer. 1

(ii) Two from:
To costly to build a physical model.
To time consuming to build a physical model.
Variables can be changed easily to see the effects of any change in input.
Dangerous
Any other suitable answer. 2

2 **(a)** One from:
Weather station.
Automatic car park.
Monitoring a scientific experiment.
Monitoring traffic.
Temperature
Any suitable answer. 1

(b) A suitable reason for using the computer in the given application such as:
not having to remember to take the readings.
automatic
more accurate readings. 1

OCR

RECOGNISING ACHIEVEMENT

Oxford Cambridge and RSA Examinations

General Certificate of Secondary Education

INFORMATION AND COMMUNICATION TECHNOLOGY A **1094**

HIGHER TIER (2357H)
PAPER 1

MARK SCHEME

Specimen Paper 2002

General Certificate of Secondary Education

GCSE Information and Communication Technology (ICT)

Centre name					
Centre number					
Candidate number					

Exam 1 Paper B

Higher Tier

Surname
Other names
Candidate signature

Time allowed: 1 hour 15 minutes

Instructions to candidates
- Write your name and other details in the spaces provided above.
- Answer **all** questions in the spaces provided.
- Do all rough work on the paper.

Information for candidates
- Each question in Section A carries 1 mark. The marks available in Section B are given in brackets at the end of each question or part-question.
- Marks will not be deducted for incorrect answers.
- In calculations show clearly how you work out your answers.
- There are 15 questions in this paper. There is one blank page.

Advice to candidates
- Work steadily through the paper.
- Don't spend too long on one question.
- If you have time at the end, go back and check your answers.

For examiner's use	Attempt Nº		
	1	2	3
Section A Total			
Q13			
Q14			
Q15			
Total 60			

Leave blank

SECTION A — each question carries one mark

1 A school keeps pupil data on a database. Access to the database is restricted by all of the following except

- **A** passwords
- **B** usernames
- **C** access rights
- **D** sequential access

Answer

2 Personalised standard letters can be created using

- **A** spreadsheet formulas
- **B** text frames
- **C** mail merge
- **D** file backups

Answer

3 The central processing unit (CPU) of a computer contains three parts known by the initials

- **A** ALU, IAS and CU
- **B** ALI, ASI and CU
- **C** ULA, ASI and UC
- **D** AUL, SIA and UC

Answer

4 A wide area network is different from a local area network because

- **A** it connects fewer computers together
- **B** it does not need a network file server to operate it
- **C** computers are not permanently connected to the network
- **D** all the computers are located in one building

Answer

Leave blank

5 An operating system can carry out all of the following tasks except

- **A** inform a user that a floppy disk is full
- **B** send a document to a printer
- **C** sort data on a database into alphabetical order
- **D** load a piece of applications software

Answer ☐

6 Data stored on a CD-ROM can be retrieved by a computer using

- **A** direct access
- **B** serial access
- **C** security access
- **D** sequential access

Answer ☐

7 A new computer system is introduced immediately after the old computer system is dismantled. This is known as

- **A** phased implementation
- **B** sequential implementation
- **C** direct implementation
- **D** parallel implementation

Answer ☐

8 A block of information placed at the bottom of every page in a document is called a

- **A** header
- **B** footer
- **C** macro
- **D** template

Answer ☐

9 A manager wishes to calculate the weekly sales total in a shop. Part of the spreadsheet is shown below.

Leave blank

	A	B	C	D	E
1	Product	Hats	Scarves	Gloves	Fish
2	Quantity sold	65	45	67	4
3	Selling price	£7.99	£3.50	£2.99	£2.50
4	Sales this week	£519.35	£157.50	£200.33	£10.00
5	Total weekly sales (all products)				

The formula that should be entered into cell B5 is

A = B4 + B3 +B2

B = Sum (B4: D4)

C = Sum (B4: E4)

D = Sum (B3:E3)*Sum (B2:E2)

Answer

10 Storing a sequence of data as comma separated variables (CSV) on a word-processed document means that

A the data can be saved as a JPEG more easily

B the data can be exported into a spreadsheet package more easily

C the data can be printed more quickly

D the data cannot be deleted

Answer

Leave blank

11 The following database shows information about staff salaries.

Surname	First name	Salary	Payroll Number	Age
Kendal	Kay	£5,600	35789	61
Kirby	Stephen	£3,800	24633	43
Morland	Wes	£4,500	57990	17
Bloodaxe	Eric	£5,600	64146	22
Kirby	Eric	£16,800	63355	17

The name of the key field in this database is

A Surname
B Salary
C Age
D Payroll number

Answer ☐

12 E-mail attachments can contain viruses. Four possible methods of preventing viruses causing damage are listed below.

1 The attachments are scanned using anti-virus software before they are downloaded onto the computer.
2 The attachments are downloaded onto a floppy disk before being transferred to the computer's hard disk.
3 The attachments are deleted instead of being downloaded onto the computer.
4 The attachments are downloaded into a folder on the hard drive that does not contain any viruses.

The TWO MAIN methods are

A 1 and 3
B 2 and 3
C 3 and 4
D 1 and 4

Answer ☐

Leave blank

SECTION B — attempt all questions in the spaces provided

13 An architect wishes to look at the effects of putting a number of computers into a single room. Each computer radiates a certain amount of heat when switched on. This heat increases the temperature of the room. A certain amount of heat is lost through the windows.

(a) The architect decides to produce a computer model of this situation using a spreadsheet.

(i) List four pieces of data that will need to be input into the computer model.

1 ....

2 ....

3 ....

4 ....

(4 marks)

(ii) List two items of output data that the architect might be able to obtain from the model.

1 ....

2 ....

(2 marks)

(b) The model can be used to carry out a 'what-if' analysis.

(i) Explain what is meant by a 'what-if' analysis.

....

....

....

....

(3 marks)

Leave blank

(ii) Explain how this particular model could be used to carry out a what-if analysis.

....

....

....

....

(3 marks)

(c) Give two reasons why the model might not produce accurate results.

Reason 1 ....

....

Reason 2 ....

....

(2 marks)

Turn over for next question.

Leave blank

14 Needham Bakeries are looking to increase the use of computers at their head office and main bakery. The bakery owners think that the existing computer system is too small.

(a) A systems analyst is asked to carry out research into the problems of the existing system.

Suggest four things that the systems analyst could do to find problems with the system.

1 ....

2 ....

3 ....

4 ....

(4 marks)

(b) The bakery wishes to set up a new database to store information about its customers.

Use the box below to design a data-capture form that the bakery could use.

(4 marks)

Leave blank

(c) The head office currently has five standalone computers. The bakery wishes to connect them together into a network.

Explain three benefits to the bakery of networking its computers.

Benefit 1 ....

....

Benefit 2 ....

....

Benefit 3 ....

....

(6 marks)

(d) The systems analyst recommends that the bakery will need a file server.

Give one function of a file server.

....

....

(1 mark)

(e) The bakery accountant is worried that confidential financial information stored on the network could be seen by unauthorised staff.

Give three security precautions that the bakery could use to prevent unauthorised access to the network.

Precaution 1 ....

....

Precaution 2 ....

....

Precaution 3 ....

....

(3 marks)

Leave blank

(f) The systems analyst recommends testing the system and writing user documentation.

(i) Explain one reason why it is important to test the new computer system.

....

....

(2 marks)

(ii) Give two types of documentation that should be written for the new computer system.

1 ....

2 ....

(2 marks)

(g) The bakery decides to install the new system using parallel implementation.

(i) Give one benefit and one drawback of parallel implementation.

Benefit ....

....

Drawback ....

....

(2 marks)

(ii) Give one other method of implementing the system.

....

(1 mark)

15 "The increased use of computers in businesses is having a major impact on the ways in which people work."

Leave blank

Discuss the above statement. Draw on any relevant knowledge in your answer.

....

....

....

....

....

....

....

....

....

....

....

....

....

....

....

....

....

....

....

....

....

(9 marks)

Leave blank

BLANK PAGE

IHP41B 1201

General Certificate of Secondary Education

GCSE Information and Communication Technology (ICT)

Centre name					
Centre number					
Candidate number					

Exam 2 Paper A

Higher Tier

Surname
Other names
Candidate signature

Time allowed: 1 hour 30 minutes

Instructions to candidates

- Write your name and other details in the spaces provided above.
- Answer **all** questions in the spaces provided.
- Do all rough work on the paper.

Information for candidates

- The marks available are given in brackets at the end of each question or part-question.
- Marks will not be deducted for incorrect answers.
- In calculations show clearly how you work out your answers.
- There are 12 questions in this paper. There are three blank pages.

Advice to candidates

- Work steadily through the paper.
- Don't spend too long on one question.
- If you have time at the end, go back and check your answers.

For examiner's use

Q	Attempt Nº 1	2	3	Q	Attempt Nº 1	2	3
1				8			
2				9			
3				10			
4				11			
5				12			
6							
7							
				Total 80			

1 Bustblockers, a chain of video stores, would like to send a letter to all of its customers who live in Kendal. The letter will tell them that a new video store has opened in their town. Customer details are stored in the firm's database.

(a) Explain how the store could obtain from its database a list of the customers who live in Kendal.

....

....

....

(3 marks)

(b) Explain how the store could then use mail merge to produce the letter.

....

....

....

....

....

(4 marks)

2 A water supply company uses a robot to travel through a pipeline and detect leaks. At one point the pipeline makes a sharp turn to the right.

(a) Describe the features of the robot that could enable it to travel along the whole length of the pipe.

....

....

....

....

....

(4 marks)

Leave blank

(b) The robot can be fitted with a camera to take photographs of the pipe. Give two benefits and two problems of using a digital camera to take the photographs.

Benefits ....

....

Problems ....

....

(4 marks)

3 Clever Tins Ltd designs and makes biscuit tins. The tins are designed using computer-aided design (CAD) software.

Give two features of CAD software that make it suitable for designing the tins.

Feature 1 ....

Feature 2 ....

(2 marks)

4 The central processing unit (CPU) of a computer system is made up of three main parts.

(a) Name the three main parts of the central processing unit.

....

....

....

(3 marks)

(b) Explain what any one of the three parts does.

....

....

....

(3 marks)

Leave blank

5 Carrie Stock runs the school tuck shop at Thrasham High. She has the following data stored on a spreadsheet:

	A	B	C	D	E	F
1	**Product name**	**Cost**	**Selling price**	**Profit per item**	**Quantity sold**	**Profit made**
2	Bear drops	£0.04	£0.07	£0.03	350	£10.50
3	Face invaders	£0.12	£0.28	£0.16	80	£12.80
4	Pa's bars	£0.24	£0.35	£0.11	55	£6.05
5	Hairy milk	£0.25	£0.33	£0.08	62	£4.96
6	Total profit made					£34.31

(a) Write out the formula that appears in cell F2.

....

(1 mark)

(b) Explain how Carrie could have used the spreadsheet's functions to quickly calculate the profit for the other sweets.

....

....

(2 marks)

(c) Carrie is told that Bear Drops actually cost 5p instead of 4p, but she still decides to charge 7p for them. She changes the data in cell B2. Which other cells will automatically change as a result?

....

....

(3 marks)

6 An airline has an internet booking facility that lets customers know how many seats are available on any given flight. When a customer makes a flight booking the number of available seats immediately reduces.

(a) What type of processing does the computer system use?

....

(1 mark)

(b) The airline is interested in knowing how many people visit its website every day. Explain how the airline can use computer software to obtain this information.

....

....

(2 marks)

Leave blank

Leave blank

(c) The website uses hyperlinks. It also contains a form where customers can enter information when they make a flight booking.

(i) Explain how a hyperlink works.

....

....
(2 marks)

(ii) Identify three pieces of information that the form might ask customers to give.

1 ....

2 ....

3 ....
(3 marks)

7 Mary would like to do her banking on the internet but is worried that other people might be able to obtain her bank account details.

(a) Identify two possible benefits to Mary of internet banking.

Benefit 1 ....

Benefit 2 ....
(2 marks)

(b) Identify two benefits to the bank if more people use the internet to do their banking.

Benefit 1 ....

Benefit 2 ....
(2 marks)

(c) Give two security measures that could help prevent unauthorised access to Mary's bank details.

Measure 1 ....

Measure 2 ....
(2 marks)

Leave blank

8 Select Holiday Cottages currently produces a printed brochure of all its properties. The brochure is produced using desktop publishing (DTP) software.

(a) Explain how desktop publishing software can be used to produce the brochure.

....

....

....

....

....
(4 marks)

Select Holiday Cottages is thinking of making its brochure available on the internet.

(b) Identify two benefits to Select Holiday Cottages of putting its property details on the internet.

Benefit 1 ....

Benefit 2 ....
(2 marks)

(c) Give one piece of hardware and two pieces of software that customers might need in order to access the property details from their computer at home.

....

....

....
(3 marks)

(d) Select Holiday Cottages has designed a company logo using graphics software. The logo is stored on the firm's computer as a bitmap file.

Explain one difference between the way that a picture is stored as a bitmap file and as a vector-based file.

....

....

....
(2 marks)

9 Kieran is designing a database for staff at a restaurant to use. He is unsure about whether to use a menu-driven user interface or a command-driven user interface.

Leave blank

(a) Give one difference between these two types of user interface.

....

....

(1 mark)

(b) Identify one benefit and one drawback of a menu-driven user interface.

Benefit ....

Drawback ....

(2 marks)

(c) Restaurant staff will enter details of customer orders onto the computer using a keyboard. Kieran is unsure about whether to use a normal (QWERTY) keyboard or a concept keyboard.

Discuss the benefits and problems of using a concept keyboard.

....

....

....

....

(4 marks)

Leave blank

10 Dan uses a sensor to measure the temperature during school sports day. He decides to take a measurement every ten minutes. He takes 30 readings in total.

(a) How long is the logging interval?

....

(1 mark)

(b) How long is the logging period?

....

(1 mark)

(c) For each example in the table below, identify a suitable sensor. The first one has been done for you.

Occasion	**Sensor**
A burglar system	Infrared detector
Switching on street lights automatically.	
Measuring noise levels in a factory.	
Measuring the amount of radioactivity in a nuclear power plant.	

(3 marks)

11 (a) Give two differences between a floppy disk and a CD-ROM.

Difference 1 ....

....

Difference 2 ....

....

(2 marks)

(b) A computer is advertised as containing 256 megabytes of random-access memory (RAM). Explain why computers need RAM.

....

....

(2 marks)

Leave blank

(c) What happens to data stored as ROM when the computer's power supply is disconnected?

....

....
(2 marks)

(d) Sometimes data files can be compressed so that they take up less memory.
Give one benefit and one problem of compressing files.

Benefit ....

Problem ....
(2 marks)

12 Discuss the health and safety implications of the use of computers in an office.

....

....

....

....

....

....

....

....

....

....

....

....

....

....
(6 marks)

Leave blank

BLANK PAGE

Leave blank

BLANK PAGE

Leave blank

BLANK PAGE

IHP42A 1201

General Certificate of Secondary Education

GCSE
Information and Communication Technology (ICT)

Centre name					
Centre number					
Candidate number					

Surname
Other names
Candidate signature

Exam 2 Paper B
Higher Tier

Time allowed: 1 hour 15 minutes

Instructions to candidates
- Write your name and other details in the spaces provided above.
- Answer **all** questions in the spaces provided.
- Do all rough work on the paper.

Information for candidates
- Each question in Section A carries 1 mark. The marks available in Section B are given in brackets at the end of each question or part-question.
- Marks will not be deducted for incorrect answers.
- In calculations show clearly how you work out your answers.
- There are 15 questions in this paper. There is one blank page.

Advice to candidates
- Work steadily through the paper.
- Don't spend too long on one question.
- If you have time at the end, go back and check your answers.

For examiner's use	Attempt Nº 1	2	3
Section A Total			
Q13			
Q14			
Q15			
Total 60			

Leave blank

SECTION A — each question carries one mark

1 Which of the following is a utility normally found in word-processing software?

- **A** virus detector
- **B** spell checker
- **C** printer driver
- **D** screensaver

Answer ☐

2 The symbol below is used in a systems flow chart.

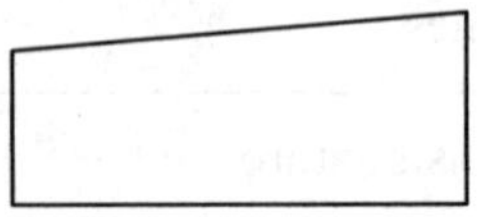

This symbol represents

- **A** backing store
- **B** computer process
- **C** manual input
- **D** paper output

Answer ☐

3 An advantage of a laptop over a desktop computer is that

- **A** laptops usually contain more memory
- **B** laptops usually have larger monitors
- **C** laptops do not require a keyboard
- **D** laptops can run on battery power

Answer ☐

4 An optical disk that can have data written onto it and deleted is called a

- **A** CD-ROM
- **B** CD-R
- **C** CD-RW
- **D** CD-RAM

Answer ☐

Leave blank

5 A doctor's surgery stores patient details on a computerised database. The database requires the patient's postcode to be entered. If the postcode is not entered an error message appears on the screen.

The database validates the postcode entry using a

A presence check
B range check
C check digit
D grammar check

Answer ☐

6 A systems analyst produces a list of objectives for a new computer system.

One reason for producing objectives is so that

A the system knows what tasks it needs to perform
B the programmer can tell when the system is built
C the performance of the system can be tested to see if it is successful
D a feasibility study can be written

Answer ☐

7 A small block of text separated from the rest of a paragraph and appearing at the top of the next page is called

A a widow
B an orphan
C a nephew
D an offspring

Answer ☐

Leave blank

8 A person who regularly types letters would write a macro in order to

A make sure that the layout of each letter is the same

B make sure that everything is spelt correctly

C reduce the time spent entering the same information on different letters

D save each file using a sensible filename

Answer ☐

9 The following spreadsheet enables an optician to see which patients require a letter reminding them to make an appointment.

	A	B	C
1	**Surname**	**Days since last appointment**	**Letter needed?**
2	Belcher	179	No
3	Wareham	181	Yes
4	Pilcher	35	No
5	Fosdyke	256	Yes

The formula used to create the display in cells C2 to C5 is an example of a

A decision function

B formatting function

C sort function

D logic function

Answer ☐

10 The spreadsheet formula C5 = (A5 * B5) + A1 contains an absolute cell reference. This means that

A the result of the formula will always be displayed as a currency

B when the formula is replicated the references to cells A5 and B5 will stay the same

C when the formula is replicated the reference to cell A1 will stay the same

D when the data in column A is sorted into numerical order the data in cell A1 will remain in A1

Answer ☐

Leave blank

11 A database with fixed-length fields

- **A** is slower to search than a database with variable-length fields
- **B** can find a record more quickly than a database with variable-length fields
- **C** can only display records containing 20 characters
- **D** cannot display a record containing fewer than 10 characters

Answer ☐

12 A counter on a web page is used to

- **A** record the total number of visits to the website
- **B** obtain personal data about the visitors to the website
- **C** enable credit card details to be transferred securely across the telephone network
- **D** prevent hackers gaining access to the HTML script for the web page

Answer ☐

Turn over for next question.

SECTION B — attempt all questions in the spaces provided

Leave blank

13 Foyle's Bank has branches in most towns and cities in Britain. All its computers are connected into a network that operates from its main computer centre in Leeds. The bank also has a number of automated teller machines (ATMs). These enable customers to withdraw cash and access their account details when there is no bank branch nearby.

(a) Bank customers are given a debit card in order to use an ATM. The debit card has a magnetic stripe on the back.

(i) Give two pieces of information contained on the magnetic stripe.

1 ....

2 ....

(2 marks)

(ii) The ATM will only issue cash to the customer if there are sufficient funds in their bank account. Explain how the bank's computer system checks this information.

....

....

....

....

(4 marks)

(b) The bank's head office computer keeps backup copies of all its computer data.

(i) Give one reason why backup data should be kept.

....

....

(1 mark)

(ii) The bank uses the ancestral method of file backup.
Explain how this method works.

....

....

....

(3 marks)

Leave blank

(c) The bank stores confidential information about staff on its network. Staff names and addresses are stored on the *staff* file. Information about wages and salaries are stored on the *payroll* file. A key field links the two files.

(i) Explain what is meant by a *key field.*

....

....

....

(2 marks)

(ii) Explain why *surname* may be an unsuitable key field.

....

....

(1 mark)

(d) Staff who use the computer system can obtain help on how to use it from manuals and online guides.

(i) Give one difference between a manual and an online guide.

....

....

(1 mark)

(ii) Give one advantage and one disadvantage of using manuals.

Advantage ....

....

Disadvantage ....

....

(2 marks)

(iii) Explain why it is important to write manuals carefully.

....

....

....

(2 marks)

Leave blank

14 A cinema uses an automated booking system. Customers can book tickets over the telephone with their credit card by keying in information using the telephone's keypad. When the customer visits the cinema they can obtain their tickets by inserting their credit card into the ticket dispenser.

(a) The computer system requires that customers use a touch-tone telephone. Explain why this is necessary.

....

....

....

(3 marks)

(b) When a customer makes a booking, the number of tickets left for a particular screening is immediately reduced. Which method of computer processing does the computer system use?

....

(1 mark)

(c) Each ticket is printed immediately before being issued to the customer. Explain how the ticket dispenser is able to print the correct information on each ticket.

....

....

....

....

(4 marks)

(d) The box below shows part of the system flow diagram for the ticket dispenser. The diagram shows how the ticket dispenser checks that the customer's credit card details are the same as the information stored on its database. If the details are the same, the tickets are printed — if not, an error message appears on the screen.

Leave blank

Complete the diagram by labelling the remaining boxes.

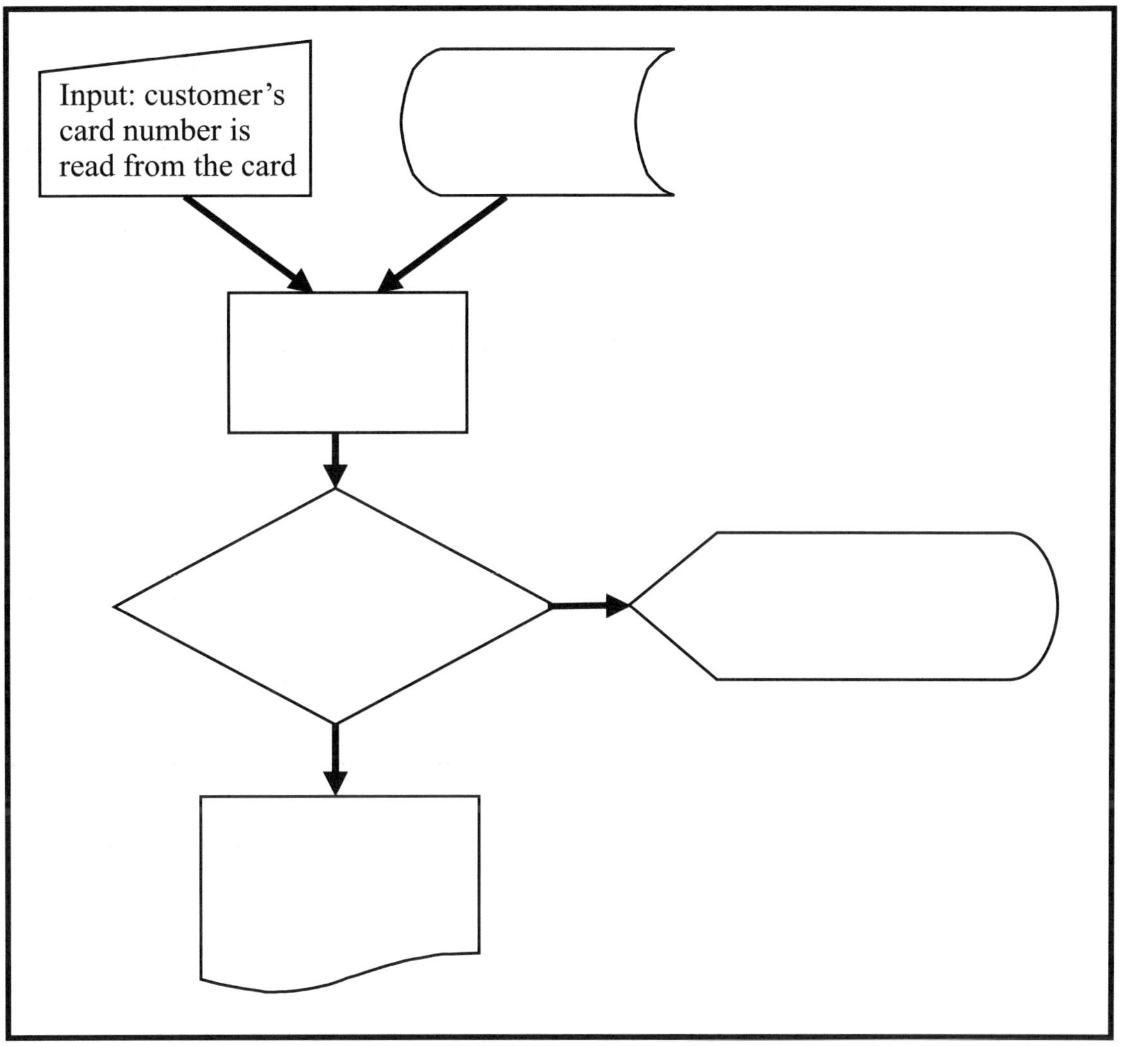

(5 marks)

Question continued overleaf.

Leave blank

(e) Explain two benefits to the customers of using the automated ticket system.

Benefit 1 ....

....

....

Benefit 2 ....

....

....

(4 marks)

(f) Explain two benefits to the cinema of using the automated ticket system.

Benefit 1 ....

....

....

Benefit 2 ....

....

....

(4 marks)

15 “There are concerns about the implications of the increased storage by organisations of personal data about people.”

Leave blank

Discuss the above statement.

....

....

....

....

....

....

....

....

....

....

....

....

....

....

....

....

....

....

....

....

(9 marks)

Leave blank

BLANK PAGE

IHP42B 1201

General Certificate of Secondary Education

GCSE Information and Communication Technology (ICT)

Centre name					
Centre number					
Candidate number					

Exam 3 Paper A

Higher Tier

Surname
Other names
Candidate signature

Time allowed: 1 hour 30 minutes

Instructions to candidates
- Write your name and other details in the spaces provided above.
- Answer **all** questions in the spaces provided.
- Do all rough work on the paper.

Information for candidates
- The marks available are given in brackets at the end of each question or part-question.
- Marks will not be deducted for incorrect answers.
- In calculations show clearly how you work out your answers.
- There are 14 questions in this paper. There are no blank pages.

Advice to candidates
- Work steadily through the paper.
- Don't spend too long on one question.
- If you have time at the end, go back and check your answers.

For examiner's use

Q	Attempt Nº 1	2	3	Q	Attempt Nº 1	2	3
1				8			
2				9			
3				10			
4				11			
5				12			
6				13			
7				14			
				Total 80			

1 Phil collects the following data from the boys in his class:

Leave blank

Name	Height (m)	Shoe size (UK standard size)
David	1.32	7
Goliath	1.99	13
Glenn	1.55	8
Andy	1.65	9
Colin	1.82	10

Phil wants to see if there is a relationship between height and shoe size.
He decides to test this by creating a graph using computer software.

(a) What type of graph would you recommend Phil to create?

....

(1 mark)

(b) Explain how Phil could use computer software to produce the graph.

....

....

....

(3 marks)

(c) Give two benefits of plotting the graph using a computer instead of drawing it by hand.

Benefit 1 ....

Benefit 2 ....

(2 marks)

2 Billy has an old colour photograph that he wants to e-mail to a friend.

(a) Name one input device he might use to convert the photograph into a digital image.

....

(1 mark)

(b) Name one piece of hardware (apart from a computer) and one piece of software he will need in order to send the photograph by e-mail.

....

....

(2 marks)

Leave blank

(c) Billy has a web-based e-mail account. All of his e-mail files are stored on the computer of his internet service provider.

Give two advantages to Billy of using web-based e-mail.

1 ....

2 ....

(2 marks)

3 Joshua uses his word processor to write his GCSE coursework.

(a) Joshua uses a number of the word processor's functions to help him improve the appearance of his work. For each feature say what it does.

(i) Spell checker

....

....

(1 mark)

(ii) Header and footer

....

....

(1 mark)

(iii) Readability score

....

....

(1 mark)

(b) In order to improve the appearance of his coursework Joshua decides to 'fully justify' the text. Explain what this feature does.

....

....

(1 mark)

Leave blank

4 A recruitment agency has seven offices in different parts of the country.
The office computers are all connected together using a wide area network (WAN).

(a) Describe how a WAN works.

....

....

(2 marks)

(b) Give one benefit to the business of using a WAN.

....

(1 mark)

(c) Every week the seven office managers hold a meeting using teleconferencing.

(i) Briefly describe how teleconferencing works.

....

....

(2 marks)

(ii) Give two benefits to the firm of using teleconferencing.

Benefit 1 ....

Benefit 2 ....

(2 marks)

5 Basham School is planning to purchase 30 laptop computers instead of building a new network computer room with 30 desktop computers.

(a) Identify two differences between a laptop computer and a desktop computer.

Difference 1 ....

....

Difference 2 ....

....

(2 marks)

Leave blank

(b) Identify two benefits to the school of using laptop computers.

Benefit 1 ....

Benefit 2 ....

(2 marks)

(c) Identify two problems to the school of using laptop computers.

Problem 1 ....

Problem 2 ....

(2 marks)

6 A library stores information about its books on a database. The table below shows some of the information in the database.

Author	**Title**	**Stock number**	**Date last loaned**	**Date returned**
Swift	Gulliver's Travels	3576	12-07-01	28-08-01
Swift	Gulliver's Travels	3577	20-07-00	30-07-00
Fast	The Joy of Fish	6783	30-06-90	01-07-90
Archer	100 Great Arrows	2469	23-06-89	28-08-92
Swift	Recipes for Children	2215	12-07-01	30-07-01

(a) Name one field in this database.

....

(1 mark)

(b) What is the name of the key field in this database?

....

(1 mark)

(c) Why is it important to have a key field?

....

....

(2 marks)

(d) Give one situation when it might be necessary to add a new record to the library database.

....

(1 mark)

(e) Give one situation when it might be necessary to modify a record in the library database.

....

(1 mark)

(f) Give one situation when it might be necessary to delete a record from the library database.

....

(1 mark)

7 A teacher sets up a spreadsheet to record examination results. The results are in percentage form. Part of the spreadsheet is shown below.

	A	**B**	**C**
1	Name	Exam Result (%)	Resit?
2	Kate Cropper	75	
3	Phil Degree	54	
4	Trevor Dury	32	
5	Anjli Hatton	89	

(a) The teacher wants to make sure that she enters the correct examination result for each pupil.

(i) Identify two validation checks the teacher could use.

Check 1 ....

Check 2 ....

(2 marks)

(ii) Give one reason why these checks might not guarantee that the data entered onto the spreadsheet is accurate.

....

....

(1 mark)

(b) In order to identify those pupils who need to resit the test the teacher enters the formula **C2 = If(B2>40, "No", "Resit")**.
What output information will be displayed in cell C2?

....

(1 mark)

Leave blank

(c) The teacher uses a password to access her files on the school computer network. She decides to change her password. The computer asks her to type in her new password twice.
Explain why the computer asks her to enter her new password twice.

....

....
(2 marks)

8 Which type of computer processing does each of the following situations use?
(Tick the appropriate box.)

	Real-time processing	**Batch-processing**
Booking an airline ticket		
Paying the weekly wages		
Monitoring the temperature inside a nuclear reactor		
Calculating gas bills		

(4 marks)

9 An airline uses a flight simulator to train its pilots.

(a) Explain the difference between a computer model and a computer simulation.

....

....

....
(2 marks)

(b) Give two benefits to the airline of using a computer simulation.

Benefit 1 ....

Benefit 2 ....
(2 marks)

(c) Give one drawback of using a computer model.

....
(1 mark)

Leave blank

10 A doctor's surgery wishes to collect information from its patients. The information will be stored on the surgery's database.

(a) Explain the difference between information and data.

....

....

....

(2 marks)

(b) Design a suitable data-capture form for the surgery in the space below.

(3 marks)

Leave blank

(c) Explain three benefits to the surgery of storing the information on a database.

Benefit 1 ....

....

Benefit 2 ....

....

Benefit 3 ....

....

(3 marks)

11 A network has a file server so data can be shared more easily.
The file server has an operating system.

(a) Give three tasks carried out by an operating system.

Task 1 ....

Task 2 ....

Task 3 ....

(3 marks)

(b) Most operating systems are 'multitasking'.

Explain what multitasking means.

....

....

....

(2 marks)

12 A friend shows you the following poster he has designed using a desktop publishing (DTP) package. He asks you to comment on its appearance.

Leave blank

Come to computer club!!

Every lunchtime

12.30-1pm

It's great fun!

Suggest three ways that the poster could be improved.

Improvement 1 ....

....

Improvement 2 ....

....

Improvement 3 ....

....

(3 marks)

13 A bank issues its customers with a chequebook. At the bottom of each cheque are printed details of the customer's bank account. This information is read by the bank's computer using a magnetic ink character recognition (MICR) system.

Leave blank

(a) Identify two pieces of information that are printed at the bottom of the cheque.

Item 1 ....

Item 2 ....

(2 marks)

(b) Give two benefits to the bank of using MICR.

Benefit 1 ....

....

Benefit 2 ....

....

(2 marks)

(c) The customer writes the amount of the cheque in words and figures. This is read by the computer using OCR software.

What do the letters OCR stand for?

....

(1 mark)

(d) The bank stores information about its customers on a database. Customer surnames are stored using a fixed-length field of 25 characters.

(i) Identify one advantage of using a fixed-length field.

....

(1 mark)

(ii) Identify two problems with using a fixed-length field.

1 ....

2 ....

(2 marks)

14 "The internet is doing society more harm than good".

Discuss the above statement.
Include in your answer any relevant moral, legal or social effects.

....

....

....

....

....

....

....

....

....

....

....

....

....

....

....

....

....

....

....

....

(6 marks)

Leave blank

IHP43A 1201

General Certificate of Secondary Education

GCSE
Information and Communication Technology (ICT)

Centre name					
Centre number					
Candidate number					

Surname
Other names
Candidate signature

Exam 3 Paper B
Higher Tier

Time allowed: 1 hour 15 minutes

Instructions to candidates
- Write your name and other details in the spaces provided above.
- Answer **all** questions in the spaces provided.
- Do all rough work on the paper.

Information for candidates
- Each question in Section A carries 1 mark. The marks available in Section B are given in brackets at the end of each question or part-question.
- Marks will not be deducted for incorrect answers.
- In calculations show clearly how you work out your answers.
- There are 15 questions in this paper. There is one blank page.

Advice to candidates
- Work steadily through the paper.
- Don't spend too long on one question.
- If you have time at the end, go back and check your answers.

For examiner's use	Attempt Nº 1	2	3
Section A Total			
Q13			
Q14			
Q15			
Total / 60			

Leave blank

SECTION A — each question carries one mark

1 One byte of data is made up of

A two bits
B four bits
C eight bits
D sixteen bits

Answer

2 The control unit of a computer's central processing unit (CPU) performs which TWO of the following tasks?

1 monitoring the hardware attached to the computer system
2 performing calculations
3 ensuring that data signals are sent to the correct location
4 storing data being used by the CPU

A 1 and 2
B 1 and 3
C 2 and 4
D 3 and 4

Answer

3 Which TWO of the following systems will use real-time processing?

1 a theatre ticket booking system that displays the number of available seats
2 a flight-simulator display responding to the movement of a joystick
3 a computer that updates and prints electricity bills
4 a system to calculating staff wages

A 1 and 2
B 2 and 3
C 2 and 4
D 3 and 4

Answer

4 A new computer system should be tested

A to find out how much it costs to build
B to make sure the input data is validated
C to make sure it does not contain any bugs
D to establish whether the users have been trained to use it properly

Answer [ ]

Leave blank

5 An advantage of a digital camera over a conventional print camera is that

A the camera does not need electrical power to operate
B the photographs can be sent to friends as e-mail attachments
C the photographs can be edited using spreadsheet formulas
D digital cameras are usually cheaper to buy than conventional film cameras

Answer [ ]

6 A shop manager wishes to calculate a running total of sales for the same products every week for a year. The formulas can be entered quickly onto a spreadsheet using the

A sort function
B replicate function
C text formatting function
D database function

Answer [ ]

7 A weather forecaster wants to produce a graph to show the maximum temperature every day in June. The most appropriate graph to use is a

A pie chart
B scatter graph
C doughnut chart
D column graph

Answer [ ]

Leave blank

8 A computer simulation is

A a computer model that contains updated formulas
B the data needed to install a computer model
C the output generated by running a computer model
D the preliminary design of a computer model

Answer

9 A benefit to a bank customer of using an automated teller machine (ATM) is that

A more staff will be employed to service the ATMs
B fewer staff are required to work in bank branches
C cash can be withdrawn when the bank is closed
D customers no longer need to remember their personal identification number (PIN)

Answer

10 The Copyright, Design and Patents Act makes it illegal to

A gain unauthorised access to a computer
B store inaccurate personal data on a computer
C copy an image from a web site and use it without acknowledging the source
D store confidential data about another person for longer than is necessary

Answer

11 Web pages can be accessed by all of the following except

A following a hypertext link
B typing the URL into the web browser address bar
C carrying out a keyword search using a search engine
D sending an e-mail to the web master

Answer

Leave blank

12 Opening a web page results in a padlock symbol being displayed on the user's web browser. This means that the web site

A uses encryption software to make online shopping safe

B does not contain any computer viruses

C can only be viewed if the correct password is entered

D will not put a cookie onto the user's computer

Answer [ ]

Turn over for next question.

Leave blank

SECTION B — attempt all questions in the spaces provided

13 Robin is a scientist employed to monitor pollution levels in a number of rivers near a large industrial town.

(a) Robin wants to design a computer system to automatically measure oxygen levels over a one-month period.

Explain how he could use data-logging equipment to do this.

....

....

....

....

....

(4 marks)

(b) Robin wants the system to be able to send a message to his mobile phone if oxygen levels fall below a certain level.

(i) Explain how he could adapt his system to do this.

....

....

....

(2 marks)

Leave blank

(ii) In the space below draw a flow chart to illustrate how the system will work.

(4 marks)

(c) Robin wishes to test his telephone warning system to see if it works.
Describe how he could do this.

....

....

....

....

....
(4 marks)

Turn over for next question.

Leave blank

14 A publishing company uses computers to create its daily newspaper. A copy of the newspaper is also made available on the internet.

(a) Explain how the editor uses desktop publishing software to create the newspaper.

....

....

....

....

....

....

....

(5 marks)

(b) Explain two ways in which the publisher benefits from using computers to create the newspaper.

Benefit 1 ....

....

Benefit 2 ....

....

(4 marks)

Leave blank

(c) Give four health and safety implications of the office being fully computerised.

1 ....

....

2 ....

....

3 ....

....

4 ....

....

(4 marks)

(d) A journalist leaves the office and writes a story using a laptop computer. The story is sent to the office as an e-mail attachment. The editor downloads the file but is unable open it.
Give two possible reasons why the file cannot be opened.

Reason 1 ....

....

Reason 2 ....

....

(2 marks)

(e) The internet version of the newspaper contains a search engine. The search engine enables users to find specific stories that the newspaper has published.

(i) Briefly describe how a search engine works.

....

....

....

....

(3 marks)

Question continued overleaf.

(ii) The publisher decides that the web site will only store copies of the newspaper that have been published in the past six months. Give two possible reasons why this decision has been made.

Reason 1 ....

....

Reason 2 ....

....

(2 marks)

(f) Both versions of the newspaper carry advertisements paid for by other businesses. Some firms choose to only advertise on the internet.

(i) Give three reasons why businesses choose to advertise on the internet.

Reason 1 ....

....

Reason 2 ....

....

Reason 3 ....

....

(3 marks)

(ii) Explain why some businesses are reluctant to put a copy of their company logo onto their internet advertisements.

....

....

....

(2 marks)

Leave blank

15 The use of computers in schools to help children learn is increasing.
Discuss the impact of this trend.

Leave blank

....

....

....

....

....

....

....

....

....

....

....

....

....

....

....

....

(9 marks)

Leav
blan

BLANK PAGE

IHP43B 1201

Coordination Group Publications

GCSE

ICT

Answer Book

GCSE Practice Papers

Higher Tier

Contents

These practice papers won't make you better at ICT...

...but they will show you what you **can** do, and what you **can't** do.

The papers are just like the ones you'll get on the day — so they'll tell you what you need to **work at** if you want to do **better**.

Do an exam, **mark it** and look at what you **got wrong**. **That's** the stuff you need to learn.

Go away, **learn** those tricky bits, then **do the same exam again**. If you're **still** getting questions wrong, you'll have to do even **more practice** and **keep testing** yourself until you get all the questions right.

It doesn't sound like a lot of **fun**, but how else do you expect to **learn** it?

There are two big ways to improve your score

1) **Keep practising the things you get wrong**
If you keep getting the database questions wrong, practise databases. If you keep making a hash of the control questions, practise control. And so on...

2) **Don't throw away easy marks**
Even if a question looks dead simple you have to check your answer and make sure it's sensible.

Doing the Exams

There are **three** sets of practice papers in this pack.
Each set contains two papers.

Paper A
1 hour 30 minutes **80 marks**

Paper B
1 hour 15 minutes **60 marks**

You should answer all of the questions.
Of course you don't **have** to answer **all** of them...
...but if you don't attempt a question you will **definitely** get zero marks for it.

So, if you're not sure of the answer, have a guess.

That way you've got a chance of getting some more marks...
...and more marks means you could get a higher grade.

Follow all the instructions

1) Make sure you know what they want you to do.
2) The most important thing is to **understand** the questions.
   Read everything really **carefully** to be sure you're doing what they want.
3) Most questions test your knowledge of ICT. They ask you to give facts about ICT, not opinions. These questions usually begin with 'Identify' or 'Give' or 'What'.
4) Some questions ask you to write about the impact of ICT on society. These questions have more marks than the other questions. They often come at the end of the paper. With these questions you get 1 mark for each point you make.

If you're going to do the practice papers more than once, then write your answers on a separate bit of paper.

Working out your grade

Do a complete exam (Paper A and Paper B).

Mark the exam papers, and add up all the marks (which gives you a mark out of 140).

Look up your total mark in this table to see what grade you got.

If you get less than a D grade on the Higher level you fail the exam.

Grade	A*	A	B	C	D
Mark out of 140	90	80	70	60	50

Important

Getting grade A, C or whatever on one of these practice papers is **no guarantee** of getting that in the real GCSE — **but** it is a pretty good guide.

GCSE ICT Higher Tier Paper 1A

1 (a) Differences include: i) ***LANs usually span a limited geographical region, e.g. within a building or buildings on the same site; WANs usually cover larger geographic regions, e.g. linking multiple sites (which might not even be in the same country)***; ii) ***LANs are permanent networks; WANs could be considered temporary networks because computers are only connected if they are 'online' at a given time***; iii) ***LANs are connected together using permanent cables; WANs need modems (or similar technology like a terminal adapter for ISDN lines, or a direct internet connection).***

Award 1 mark for each of two correct differences.

(b) (i) Answers include: i) ***a ring network is like a line network, but with the ends connected together forming a "ring"***; ii) ***this means that all the data can flow in one direction***; iii) ***on a line network, data has to flow in both directions along the cable***; iv) ***as a result, ring networks are faster***; v) ***although they often require more cable, making them more expensive***.

Award 1 mark for each of two correct points.

(ii) Benefits include: i) ***cheap to expand***; ii) ***data flows quickly around the network***; iii) ***a ring network can be resilient to any single failure***; iv) ***any inactive stations are bypassed***; v) ***more efficient use of bandwidth.***

Drawbacks include: i) ***a problem in one part of the network (e.g. damage to the network cable) may cause the whole network to fail***; ii) ***the interface cards are expensive***; iii) ***the 'T' shaped network connectors are prone to damage.***

Award 1 mark for a correct benefit and 1 mark for a correct drawback.

(c) Answers include: i) ***to prevent unauthorised access by someone who has discovered the pupil's password***; ii) ***to reduce the chances of someone discovering the pupil's password***.

Award 1 mark for one correct reason.

2 (a) ***Automated (or automatic) teller (or telling) machine.***

Award 1 mark if all three parts have been correctly given.

(b) The following sequence of events will take place: i) ***the customer inserts their bank card into the ATM***; ii) ***the ATM will read the card details on the magnetic stripe on the back of the card***; iii) ***the machine asks the customer to key in their personal identification number (PIN)***; iv) ***the PIN is read by the ATM which verifies that the customer is entitled to use the card and withdraw cash***; v) ***the customer keys in the amount of cash to be withdrawn***; vi) ***the ATM counts and issues the required amount of cash and sends an instruction to the customer's bank to reduce the customer's bank balance.***

Award 1 mark for each of three correctly identified events.

(c) ***Electronic funds transfer at (the) point of sale.***

Award 2 marks if all the parts are correctly identified. Award 1 mark if either 'electronic funds transfer' or 'point of sale' is correct.

(d) Answers include: i) ***verification of a personal identification number***; ii) ***asking the customer to sign credit/debit card receipts***; iii) ***putting an expiry date onto each card. Each of these methods helps to reduce fraud by making it harder for someone to use a stolen card***.

Award 1 mark for identifying a correct method and 1 mark for saying how it can help reduce card fraud.

3 Benefits include: i) ***documents take up less storage space than a paper-based system of filing cabinets***; ii) ***it is quicker to locate a specific piece of information***; iii) ***information on the properties can be edited more quickly than with a paper-based system***.

Award 1 mark for each of two correct benefits.

4 (a) Answers include ***temperature sensor*** or ***thermistor***. Do not allow 'thermometer'. Some air-conditioning systems adjust for humidity so allow ***humidity sensor***.

Award 1 mark for an appropriate and correctly named sensor.

(b) Answers include: i) ***the temperature sensor measures the temperature inside the car***; ii) ***the reading is compared with the target temperature of 21 degrees Celsius (or a range of, say, 1 °C either side of this)***; iii) ***if the temperature is above the target temperature (or range) an output signal is sent to an output device (refrigeration device) to cool the air***; iv) ***if the temperature is below the target temperature (or range) an output signal switches on the air-conditioning heater***; v) ***the temperature is measured again following the adjustment (either at regular intervals or continuously), and the whole procedure repeated (an example of a feedback loop).***

Award 1 mark for each of four correct points.

5 Jane should i) ***enter the results onto a spreadsheet making sure that each item of data is entered into a separate cell***; ii) ***a formula should be entered into a fourth column to calculate the difference between column 3 ("End of Reign") and column 2 ("Start of Reign")***; iii) ***this formula can be copied down the column***; iv) ***the data to be graphed can then be highlighted and the graph created***; v) ***the graph should be a bar graph with 'King' on the horizontal (x) axis and 'Length of Reign' on the vertical (y) axis***.

Award 1 mark for each of four correct points.

6 (a) Answers are: ***thermistor***; ***keyboard***; ***pressure sensor***.

Award 1 mark for each correct answer.

(b) Answers are: ***graph plotter***; ***VDU***.

Award 1 mark for each correct answer.

Note: central processing unit is neither an input or output device.

7 (a) Data encryption is i) ***when data is converted using a special code***; ii) ***this data can only be decoded by using the right encryption software***; iii) ***encryption software is used to transmit confidential information, such as credit card details, on the internet***.

Award 1 mark for each of two correct points.

(b) (i) Answers include: i) ***Repetitive-strain injury (RSI)***; ii) ***headaches***; iii) ***eye strain***; iv) ***back strain***; v) ***other aches (e.g. shoulders)***; vi) ***tendonitis (e.g. in wrists).***

Award 1 mark for each of two correct points.

(ii) Answers include: i) ***take regular breaks away from the computer***; ii) ***ensure good background lighting***; iii) ***fit an anti-screen-glare device***; iv) ***have regular eye checks***; v) ***use a good computer chair***; vi) ***sit properly at the workstation***; vii) ***use an ergonomic keyboard (designed to put less strain on the wrists/be more comfortable to use)***; viii) ***reduce the amount of time spent at the computer***; ix) ***use voice-recognition software to reduce her need for the keyboard***, x) ***use a good quality monitor with high refresh rate***.

Award 1 mark for each of two correct points.

8 (a) Contents should include: ***name (first and last)***; ***address***; ***telephone number(s)***; ***health information (e.g. allergies)***; ***date of birth***.

Award 1 mark for each of three pieces of relevant information.
Award 1 mark if the layout of the form is appropriate (e.g. the form should give boxes with space for a fixed maximum number of characters, and where possible tick boxes should be used).

(b) Answers include: i) ***the DTP software is used to combine information produced in other programs***; ii) ***text and tables can be produced using a word processor***; iii) ***graphs of pupil results are produced using a spreadsheet and graphing software***; iv) ***images can be taken from a clip art library; digital photographs or prints which have been scanned can be manipulated using photo-editing software***; v) ***the DTP program can be used to improve the layout of the newsletter***; vi) ***the newsletter can be printed using a high quality colour printer***; vii) ***the newsletter could be e-mailed to parents***.

Award 1 mark for each of six correct points.

9 (a) Answers include: i) ***temperatures are collected by a temperature sensor*** (or thermistor, do not accept thermometer); ii) ***readings are taken at set intervals decided by Megan (the logging interval)***; iii) ***readings are downloaded onto the computer for storage***; iv) ***at the end of the four days (the logging period) the system stops collecting readings***.

Award 1 mark for each of three correct points.

(b) Answers include: i) ***the data collected can be exported into a spreadsheet***; ii) ***the data can then be analysed using formulas***; iii) ***the data can be used to produce a graph***; iv) ***the findings can then be written up using a word processor***.

Award 1 mark for each of two correct points.

10 (a) Restrictions include: i) ***data must not be processed without good reason***; ii) ***only relevant data should be collected and used***; iii) ***data must be accurate and up to date***; iv) ***data that is no longer needed should be deleted***; v) ***data holders should protect the data against theft or corruption***.

Award 1 mark for each of three correct restrictions. This question is about the Data Protection Act; references to other laws should not be given marks.

(b) Restrictions from the Computer Misuse Act include: i) ***mustn't access data you're not authorised to see (hacking)***; ii) ***mustn't make unauthorised changes to computer files (e.g. viruses or carrying out fraud)***.

Restrictions from the Copyright, Designs and Patents Act include: i) ***must not use software without the proper license***; ii) ***mustn't copy or download images and use them without permission or acknowledging the source***.

Award 1 mark for each of three correct points.

References to any other laws should not be awarded marks.

11 (a) Answers include: i) ***name***; ii) ***age***; iii) ***position***; iv) ***club***.

Award 1 mark for each of four suitable field names.
Other sensible answers are acceptable.

(b) Answers include: i) ***commonly used and understood information could be abbreviated***; ii) ***for example a goalkeeper's position could be abbreviated to GK***; iii) ***this reduces the number of characters needed to store the position from 10 to 2***.

Award 1 mark for each of two correct points.

12 (a) Answers include: i) ***a virus is a computer program***; ii) ***it can spread by copying itself/being copied from computer to computer (e.g. on a network or by means of a floppy disk)***; iii) ***it can 'infect' or 'hide in' another computer program or file (including e-mail messages)***; iv) ***it can corrupt or delete data stored on the computer's hard drive***; v) ***this can cause either hardware or software to fail to operate properly***; vi) ***this can result in the loss or damage of important data***.

Award 1 mark for each of two correct points.

(b) Answers include: i) ***she could use an anti-virus utility program***; ii) ***this is software that can scan computer files to see if they contain known viruses***; iii) ***if the attachment contains a virus the anti-virus software could clean the file by removing and deleting the virus***.

Award 1 mark for a correct point.

(c) (i) Answers include: i) ***make sure that the photograph is stored on her computer***; ii) ***connect to the internet***; iii) ***open her e-mail software program or her web-based e-mail account***; iv) ***prepare to send a new e-mail by inserting her aunt's e-mail address in the 'To' box***; v) ***select the photograph file and attach it to the e-mail message***; vi) ***press 'send'***.

Award 1 mark for each of three correct points.

(ii) Benefits include: i) ***e-mail is much quicker than sending documents by post***; ii) ***multiple copies of the same message can be sent to groups of people***; iii) ***can be used to send attachments***; iv) ***can be cheaper than using a postal service***.

(iii) Problems include: i) ***expensive to buy a computer just to send and receive e-mail***; ii) ***can only send to people with e-mail accounts***; iii) ***you must know their e-mail address, and it must be letter-perfect or it won't get there***; iv) ***reliant on the internet working properly***; v) ***relies on the other person checking their e-mail account***; vi) ***e-mail can be intercepted and read by others without you knowing.***

Award 1 mark for each of two correct benefits and 1 mark for each of two correct problems.

13 Benefits include: i) ***greater access to information***; ii) ***ability to shop from home***; iii) ***ability to bank/pay bills etc. from home***; iv) ***greater ability to work from home***; v) ***able to communicate with a wider group of people via e-mail, internet chat rooms and newsgroups***; vi) ***businesses able to sell their products worldwide***.

Problems include: i) ***easier for people to access material such as pornography***; ii) ***viruses can be transmitted across the internet***; iii) ***people without access to the technology are excluded from the benefits***; iv) ***small businesses can suffer***; v) ***makes certain crimes easier (including organised crime)***; vi) ***may help to increase the pace of life/accelerate globalisation***; vii) ***people can become 'addicted' to the internet (it can take over people's lives).***

Award 1 mark for each of six sensible and relevant points. Award a maximum of four points if only the benefits or problems are discussed.

GCSE ICT Higher Tier Paper 1B

Section A multiple choice answers

1	D
2	C
3	A
4	C
5	C
6	A
7	C
8	B
9	C
10	B
11	D
12	A

Section B

13 (a) (i) Answers include: i) ***number of computers in the room***; ii) ***number of computers switched on***; iii) ***background temperature of the room***; iv) ***external temperature***; v) ***number/area of windows***; vi) ***rate of heat loss through windows***. vii) ***size of room***.

Award 1 mark for each of four correct items of data.

(ii) Answer includes: i) ***temperature of the room***; ii) ***heat gain due to computers***; iii) ***heat loss through each window***.

Award 1 mark for each of two correct answers.

(b) (i) Answers include: i) ***a what-if analysis can be used to make predictions based on a computer model***; ii) ***it can also be used to investigate the behaviour of the model***; iii) ***the input data can be altered to see the impact of these changes on the output data***; iv) ***the rules governing the model (equations/formulas etc.) can also be changed and their impact on the output data examined***.

Award 1 mark for each of three correct points.

(ii) Answers include the following types of what-if analysis: i) ***the impact of changing the number of computers on the temperature of the room***; ii) ***the impact of changing the number of windows***; iii) ***the impact of changes in the background/external temperature of the room on the amount of heat gain***; iv) ***the impact of changing the size or type of window, e.g. installing double-glazing***.

Award 1 mark for each of three correct points.

(c) Answers include: i) ***the rules governing the behaviour of the model might be incorrect, for example the formulas might be wrong***; ii) ***the model might not include all relevant factors, for example the building might lose heat through the walls as well***; iii) ***the input data might be inaccurate***.

Award 1 mark for each of two correct points.

14 (a) Answers include: i) ***interview users***; ii) ***design/analyse questionnaires***; iii) ***observe people using the system***; iv) ***try using the system***; v) ***analyse documents such as reports and printed output***.

Award 1 mark for each of four correct points.

(b) Information requested can include: i) ***name***; ii) ***address***; iii) ***telephone number***; iv) ***products to be ordered***; v) ***payment details (e.g. credit card number).***

Award 1 mark for each of three pieces of relevant information. Award 1 mark if the layout of the form is appropriate (e.g. the form should give boxes with space for a fixed maximum number of characters, and where possible tick boxes should be used).

(c) Benefits include: i) ***peripherals such as printers can be shared; this saves money***; ii) ***software can be shared amongst different users***; iii) ***possible to communicate across the network, e.g. by intranet or shared files***.

Award 2 marks for each of three benefits. For 2 marks the benefit to the business must be made clear. Otherwise award just 1 mark.

(d) Answers include: ***file servers are used to store programs and files that can be accessed from anywhere on the network***.

Award 1 mark for one correct point.

(e) Answers include: i) ***limit access rights to certain users, e.g. so that accounts staff cannot see personnel files***; ii) ***put password protection on certain files, so that only people who know the passwords can use them***; iii) ***limit the software that individual users can operate***; iv) ***protect certain programs so that passwords are needed to run them***.

Award 1 mark for each of three correct points.

(f) (i) Answers include: i) ***to make sure that programs work and are bug free***; ii) ***otherwise the system might fail and cost the business money***, iii) ***To ensure the correct data is held against the correct person (otherwise, the consequences could be incorrect salary payments, or disclosure of private information to others)***.

Award 1 mark for recognising the need to make sure the system works. Award 2 marks for also recognising the consequences of running a system that does not work properly.

(ii) Answers include: i) ***user guides***; ii) ***installation guides***; iii) ***technical manuals***; iv) ***problem-solving guides***.

Award 1 mark for each of two correct points.

(g) (i) Benefits include: i) ***the new system is installed in one go, so problems can be sorted out quickly***; ii) ***the old system is kept operating, so it can continue to perform whilst problems with the new system are solved***.

Problems include: i) ***all tasks need to be done twice, once on the old system and once on the new system***; ii) ***this can be very costly and time consuming for staff***.

Award 1 mark for one correct benefit and 1 mark for one correct drawback.

(g) (ii) Answers include: i) ***direct implementation*** (new system directly replaces old system); ii) ***phased implementation*** (new one brought in gradually as the old system is withdrawn).

Award 1 mark for one correct method.

15 Answers include:

i) ***computers are making some jobs redundant, e.g. clerical work and office filing***;

ii) ***computers are increasing the demand for other jobs, e.g. computer programmers and operators***;

iii) ***computers increase the risk of some health and safety problems, e.g. headaches, eye strain, repetitive-strain injury (RSI), back problems***;

iv) ***computers enable more people to work from home or out of the office (teleworking)***;

v) ***this can have benefits (more time at home and with family, less commuting)***;

vi) ***and problems (less social contact, increased feeling of isolation)***;

vii) ***e-mail and text messaging are increasing the speed with which people can communicate with each other***.

viii) ***this has benefits (increased efficiency)***;

ix) ***and problems (faster pace of working life, increased stress)***.

Award 1 mark for each of nine relevant points.

GCSE ICT Higher Tier Paper 2A

1 (a) Answers include: i) ***search the database for all customers who live in Kendal***; ii) ***use suitable search criteria, for example 'Town = Kendal'***; iii) ***display the results of the search on the screen or as a printed report***.

Award 1 mark for each of three correct points.

(b) Answers include: i) ***create a data file containing the names and addresses of all the customers who live in Kendal***; ii) ***create a standard (form) letter using word-processing software***; iii) ***insert field codes (e.g. <name>) into the form letter***; iv) ***run the mail merge to merge the standard letter and the data file together***; v) ***print the letters***.

Award 1 mark for each of four correct points.

2 (a) Answers include: i) ***the robot will need to be either flexible or very short to get around the corner***; ii) ***the robot could have a sensor or video camera to detect whether it can move forwards or it has hit a wall***; iii) ***the robot will process the data and continue to move forward until it hits a wall***; iv) ***alternatively it might be remote controlled***; v) ***the robot will need a communication link if it is remote controlled (e.g. it might be connected by a cable)***; vi) ***the robot could have output devices such as actuators to change direction and move forward***; vii) ***the robot will need a reverse gear or will need to be able to turn around.***

Award 1 mark for each of four correct points. Other answers are possible.

(b) Benefits include: i) ***images can be stored digitally***; ii) ***images can be viewed immediately***; iii) ***images can be transmitted to remote viewers, for example via e-mail***; iv) ***digital cameras are cheaper to operate (you don't have to buy film).***

Problems include: i) ***digital cameras use energy, so would need batteries or an external electricity supply***; ii) ***digital images take up a large amount of computer memory***; iii) ***digital cameras are more expensive***; ii) ***the image might be less detailed than with a conventional camera.***

Award 1 mark for each of two benefits and 1 mark for each of two problems.

3 Answers include: i) ***can see what a tin will look like before it is made (or without having to make it)***; ii) ***images can be rotated so the object can be viewed from any angle***; iii) ***different projections of the object can be created automatically***; iv) ***software can generate costings automatically***.

Award 1 mark for each of two correct points.

4 (a) Answers are: ***control unit***; ***arithmetic and logic unit***; ***immediate access store***.

Award 1 mark for each correctly named component.

(b) Answers for control unit include: i) ***coordinates the work of the whole computer system***; ii) ***controls and monitors hardware***; iii) ***controls the flow of data***; iv) ***controls the flow of input and output signals***.

Answers for the arithmetic and logic unit include: i) ***processes data by modifying it***; ii) ***for example by performing a calculation based on a set of data***; iii) ***makes decisions based on logical instructions***; iv) ***deciding if a piece of data meets a certain criteria***; v) ***for example deciding whether the temperature of a room exceeds a specified tolerance***.

Answers for the immediate access store include: i) ***temporarily stores data being used by the computer***; ii) ***for example a document being created by the user***; iii) ***any data in the immediate access store is volatile; a loss of electrical power will result in the data being lost***.

Award 1 mark for each of three correct points. All of the three points must relate to the same CPU component.

5 (a) Answer is ***D2*E2***.

Award 1 mark for correct formula.

(b) Answers include: i) ***copy down the formula from F2 into the other cells***; ii) ***use copy and paste***; iii) ***use replication***.

Award 1 mark for the idea of copying the formula and 1 mark for using a technical term.

(c) Answer is ***D2, F2 and F6***.

Award 1 mark for each correct cell.

6 (a) Answer is ***real-time processing***.

1 mark for correct answer.

(b) Answers include: i) ***using a web counter***; ii) ***this records how many 'hits' or 'visits' are made to the web site***; iii) ***a cookie (text file) can be put onto the visitor's computer to make sure that they are not counted each time they visit the site***.

Award 1 mark for each of two correct points.

(c) (i) Answers include: i) ***a hyperlink is an instruction to the computer to open a specific file or web page***; ii) ***when the user clicks on the hyperlink the computer locates and opens the specified file or web page***.

Award 1 mark for each of two correct points.

(ii) Answers include: i) ***name***; ii) ***address***; iii) ***e-mail address***; iv) ***whether single or return is wanted***; v) ***class of travel (e.g. standard or business class)***; vi) ***date of travel/date of return***; vii) ***place of departure/ destination***.

Award 1 mark for each of three correct points.

7 (a) Benefits to Mary include: i) ***can access bank account details from home***; ii) ***can access details 24 hours a day***; iii) ***can take more control of her own bank account***; iv) ***internet banks often offer a better rate of interest/ lower charges***.

Award 1 mark for each of two correct points.

(b) Benefits to the bank include: i) ***fewer bank branches are needed***; ii) ***fewer employees are needed***; iii) ***fewer staff and branches means lower business costs for the bank.***

Award 1 mark for each of two correct points.

(c) Answers include: i) ***use of username and password***; ii) ***additional security features such as date of birth, mother's maiden name etc.***; iii) ***use of data encryption software***; iv) ***use of a digital certificate.***

Award 1 mark for each of two correct points.

8 (a) Answers include: i) ***the DTP software is used to combine information produced in other programs***; ii) ***text and tables can be produced using a word processor***; iii) ***images can be taken from a clip art library***; ***digital photographs or prints which have been scanned can be manipulated using photo-editing software***; v) ***the DTP program can be used to improve the layout of the brochure***; vi) ***the brochure can be printed using a high quality colour printer***.

Award 1 mark for each of four correct points.

(b) Answers include: i) ***can be cheaper than mailing printed copies to people***; ii) ***the brochure can be kept up to date more easily***; iii) ***the brochure can be available to more people***; iv) ***the brochure is available instantly; you don't have to wait for the post.***

Award 1 mark for each of two correct benefits.

(c) Hardware includes: i) ***modem***; ii) ***terminal adapter (e.g. for ISDN line)***; iii) ***a direct internet connection.***

Software includes: i) ***web browser***; ii) ***dialling software to contact an internet service Provide (ISP)***.

Award 1 mark for one correct piece of hardware and 1 mark for each of two correct pieces of software.

(d) Answers include: i) ***each part of the graphic on a bitmap file (each pixel) is stored as an individual item of data, a vector based graphic saves a line as an equation***; ii) ***bitmap files tend to use more memory than a vector-based file***.

Award 2 marks for explaining how the two file types are different. Award only 1 mark for identifying a relevant feature of one of the file types.

9 (a) Differences include: i) ***menu-driven interfaces display a list of options, command-driven interfaces display a space for a prompt or command***; ii) ***menu driven systems ask the user to select a command by using the mouse or a keyboard short cut, command-driven interfaces require the user to type in an instruction***.

Award 1 mark for a correct difference. A statement of a feature of one system that fails to compare it with the other should be given no mark.

(b) Benefits include: i) ***command-driven systems require the user to memorise all the commands; menu driven systems don't***.

Problems include: i) ***command-driven systems can be quicker to operate than menu driven systems, providing you have learned all the commands***.

Award 1 mark for a correct benefit and 1 mark for a correct problem.

(c) Benefits include: i) ***good for repetitive entering of the same information***; ii) ***can reduce the number of input instructions given***; ii) ***can be quicker once the keyboard is learnt.***

Problems can include: i) ***only allows a limited amount of information to be entered***; ii) ***easier to enter incorrect information by pressing the wrong key***.

Award 1 mark for each of four correct points. Award a maximum of 3 marks if only benefits or problems are covered.

10 (a) Answer is ***10 minutes***.
Award 1 mark for correct answer.

(b) Answer is ***5 hours*** (or ***300 minutes***).
Award 1 mark for correct answer.

(c) Answers are: i) ***light sensor (e.g. light-dependent resistor (LDR))***; ii) ***sound/noise detector (or microphone)***; iii) ***radioactivity detector/ Geiger counter/Geiger-Müller tube***.
Award 1 mark for each correct point.

11 (a) Differences include: i) ***a CD-ROM can hold more data than a floppy disk***; ii) ***a floppy disk can have its data deleted and new data written on them; a CD-ROM can't***; iii) ***a floppy disk has a built-in protective cover; a CD-ROM doesn't.***

Award 1 mark for each of two correct differences.

(b) Reasons include i) ***to store data that is being used temporarily by a program or the CPU***; ii) ***to enable programs to be run more quickly***; iii) ***for screen memory.***

Award 1 mark for each of two correct points.

(c) Answers include: i) ***ROM is permanent memory***; ii) ***so when the power supply is lost the data is retained***.

Award 1 mark for each of two correct points.

(d) Benefits include: i) ***compressed files take up less permanent memory (e.g. disk space)***; ii) ***more files can be stored on a storage device***; iii) ***large files can be sent across the internet more quickly***; iv) ***files might fit onto a floppy disk etc. that wouldn't fit if they weren't compressed.***

Problems include: i) ***need decompression software to open the files***; ii) ***having to decompress files means extra hassle***; iii) ***viruses might more easily be hidden in compressed files.***

Award 1 mark for a correct benefit and 1 mark for a correct problem.

12 Answers include:

Increased risks of the following health hazards: i) ***Repetitive-strain injury (RSI)***; ii) ***headaches***; iii) ***eye strain***; iv) ***back strain***; v) ***other aches (e.g. shoulders)***; vi) ***tendonitis (e.g. in wrists).***

Users might take the following precautions: i) ***take regular breaks away from the computer***; ii) ***ensure good background lighting***; iii) ***fit an anti-screen-glare device***; iv) ***have regular eye checks***; v) ***use a good computer chair***; vi) ***sit properly at the workstation***.

Need for employers to take into account health and safety legislation, for example i) ***Health and Safety at Work Act***; ii) ***Display Screen Equipment Regulations 1992***.

This requires them to: i) ***provide decent lighting***; ii) ***give regular breaks***; iii) ***provide free eye tests***; iv) ***provide health and safety advice and training***.

Award 1 mark for each of six relevant points.

You are mainly being tested on your knowledge of relevant issues.
You will not be tested on your ability to develop a good written argument.

GCSE ICT Higher Tier Paper 2B

Section A multiple choice answers

1	B
2	C
3	D
4	C
5	A
6	C
7	B
8	C
9	D
10	C
11	B
12	A

Section B

13 (a) (i) Answers include: i) ***customer account number***; ii) ***bank sort code***; iii) ***card number***.

Award 1 mark for each of two correct points.

(ii) Answers include: i) ***the ATM reads the customer's account details from the customer's cash card***; ii) ***the customer keys in the amount to be withdrawn***; iii) ***the bank's computer system obtains the amount the customer can withdraw from its database***; iv) ***the amount to be withdrawn is compared with the amount in the account***; v) ***the ATM is instructed either to issue the cash or to tell the customer that they do not have sufficient funds***.

Award 1 mark for each of four correct points.

(b) (i) Answers include: i) ***in case data is accidentally or deliberately deleted***; ii) ***in case data is accidentally or deliberately amended or corrupted***; iii) ***in case data is lost (e.g. from damage to/theft of computer system)***; iv) ***in case past data is needed to help detect fraud.***

Award 1 mark for one correct point.

(ii) Answers include: i) ***the most recent backup copy is called the son***; ii) ***when the next backup copy is made the son becomes the father copy***; iii) ***when the next backup is made the father copy becomes the grandfather copy***; iv) ***when the next backup copy is made the grandfather copy is deleted***.

Award 1 mark for each of three correct points.

(c) (i) Answers include: i) ***the key field is a field that contains no two records the same***; ii) ***it can be used to identify a specific record***; iii) ***for example a payroll number in an employee database or a pupil number in a school database***.

Award 1 mark for each of two correct points.

(ii) Answers include: i) ***because two or more people can share the same surname***; ii) ***because a search for a particular surname might bring up more than one person***.

Award 1 mark for one correct point.

(d) (i) Differences include: i) ***manuals are paper-based; online guides are stored digitally***; ii) ***online guides can be interactive; manuals cannot interact***.

Award 1 mark for one correct difference.

(ii) Benefits include: i) ***can be portable***; ii) ***do not need to be connected to a computer to use it***; iii) ***some people find them quicker to scan for specific information***; iv) ***you don't have to be computer literate to use a manual***; v) ***easier to read/less chance of eye strain.***

Problems include: i) ***can be big and bulky***; ii) ***some people find it difficult to locate specific information***; iii) ***harder to keep up to date than an online guide***; iv) ***cannot do a quick search***; v) ***cannot be interactive/no hyperlinks.***

Award 1 mark for one correct benefit and 1 mark for one correct problem.

(iii) Answers include: i) ***so that people find them easy to read and understand***; ii) ***for example by avoiding unnecessary technical terms***; iii) ***so that people can quickly find the information they want***; iv) ***otherwise they fail to meet their purpose which is to act as a substitute for the help and advice of an expert***.

Award 2 marks for an answer that explains the benefits to the user of a well-written manual. Otherwise award 1 mark for one correct point.

14 (a) Answers include: i) ***the touch-tone telephone will communicate data to the automated booking system***; ii) ***each key on the telephone pad emits a different sound (different pitch)***; iii) ***the automated booking system receives this data as an input signal***; iv) ***non-touch-tone telephones are unable to provide the automated booking system with the input signals it is designed to receive***.

Award 3 marks for an answer that shows a clear understanding of how a touch-tone telephone works (points i)-iii)) as well as an understanding of why non touch-tone telephones will not provide the required input signal (point iv)). Otherwise award 1 mark for each of two correct points.

(b) Answer is ***real-time processing***.

Award 1 mark for correct answer.

(c) Answers include: i) ***when the customer inserts their credit card into the machine the card number is read by the machine***; ii) ***this number is then matched with the number in the booking system's database***; iii) ***data from the customer's booking record is then merged with the ticket master file***; iv) ***the tickets are then printed and issued to the customer***.

Award 1 mark for each of four points.

(d)

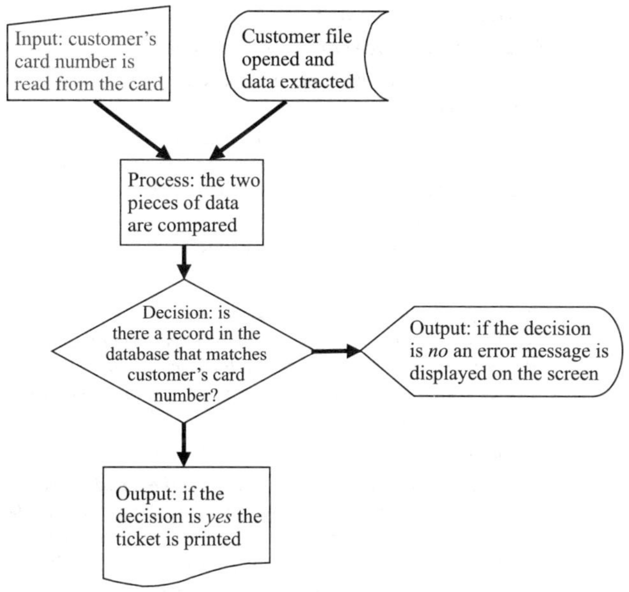

Award 1 mark for each correct box (except the one given in the question). Other answers are possible.

(e) Benefits to customers include: i) ***can book tickets from home which increases convenience;*** ii) ***customers can arrive later as they don't have to queue to buy tickets***; iii) ***it reduces the queue sizes at the cinema as less people need to queue to purchase tickets***.

Award 1 mark for each of two benefits and 1 mark for each explanation of the benefit.

(f) Benefits to the cinema include: i) ***fewer booking staff needed, so it reduces costs for the cinema***; ii) ***can offer customers a better service - more choice, shorter queuing times, which could improve cinema's popularity***.

Award 1 mark for each of two correct benefits to the cinema and 1 mark for each explanation of the benefit.

15 Relevant points include:

i) ***concerns that the data may not be accurate***;

ii) ***concerns that the data may be used to send unsolicited junk mail***;

iii) ***concerns that the Data Protection Act may not be sufficient***;

iv) ***concerns that internet cookies store information about visits to web sites***;

v) ***concerns that the government can intercept e-mail communications***;

vi) ***concerns that the data may be sold to other less scrupulous organisations***;

vii) ***concerns about the vulnerability of the data to hackers and viruses***;

viii) ***concerns about liberty, personal freedom, privacy and rights***;

ix) ***but there are benefits, e.g. spending data can be used to inform people of products they might be interested in***;

Award 1 mark for each of nine relevant points. Examples/expansion of an idea count as additional points.

GCSE ICT Higher Tier Paper 3A

1 (a) Answer is ***scatter graph*** (or ***scatterplot***).

1 mark for the correct name.

(b) Answer includes: i) ***highlight the data to go into the graph***; ii) ***select the type of graph to be produced by the software***; iii) ***select the data to go onto the vertical (y) and horizontal (x) axes***; iv) ***give the chart an appropriate title and legend***; v) ***format the text on the graph, for example the titles***.

Award 1 mark for each of three correct points.

(c) Benefits include: i) ***it is quicker***; ii) ***more professional looking***; iii) ***more accurate***; iv) ***different types of graph can be quickly generated***; v) ***changes to the data can result in the graph being automatically updated***.

Award 1 mark for each of two correct points.

2 (a) Answer is ***scanner***.

Award 1 mark for correct answer.

(b) Hardware includes: i) ***modem***; ii) ***terminal adapter (for ISDN line)***; iii) ***direct internet connection.***

Software includes: i) ***web browser***; ii) ***e-mail software***.

Award 1 mark for one correct piece of hardware and 1 mark for one correct piece of software.

(c) Benefits include: i) ***messages and attachments are stored on his web-based e-mail provider's system, freeing up memory space on his own computer***; ii) ***the e-mail account can be accessed from any device connected to the internet***.

Award 1 mark for each of two correct points.

3 (a) (i) Answers include: i) ***a spell checker checks each word against a list of words in the computer's dictionary***; ii) ***words that the computer doesn't recognise are indicated to the user***; iii) ***some spell checkers can automatically change misspelt words and/or offer a list of correctly spelt alternatives***.

Award 1 mark for one relevant feature correctly identified.

(ii) Answers include: i) ***a header is a space at the top of the page where information can be put that does not form part of the main text***; ii) ***the same information can be put at the bottom of the page (called a footer)***; iii) ***for example the date, page number or the filename of the document***; iv) ***information put into the header or footer can automatically appear on every page***; v) ***page numbers will automatically change as more pages are added***.

Award 1 mark for one relevant feature correctly identified.

(iii) Answers include: i) ***readability scores indicate how easy or difficult a document is to read***; ii) ***things like the length of each sentence are taken into account***; iii) ***the lower the score the easier the document is to read***.

Award 1 mark for one relevant feature correctly identified.

(b) Answers include: i) ***'fully justify' the text means to adjust the text so that every line begins at the left-hand margin and ends at the right-hand margin***; ii) ***a block of text is laid out like a rectangle***; iii) ***this makes the document look more professional and can be easier to read***.

Award 1 mark for one correct point.

4 (a) Answers include: i) ***computers in different offices are not permanently connected together***; ii) ***when a temporary connection is needed the computers can be connected together using modems or similar technology***; iii) ***when the connection is no longer needed the network connection is closed down***.

Award 1 mark for each of two correct points.

(b) Benefits include: i) ***a WAN makes it much easier to communicate/share data between offices***; ii) ***WANs can be cheaper than permanent connections because less cable is needed***; iii) ***WANs are more flexible; it is easier to connect new offices to a WAN than a LAN***.

Award 1 mark for one correct benefit.

(c) (i) Answers include: i) ***computers are connected together across a network (e.g. a WAN or the internet)***; ii) ***each computer needs a camera, a microphone and software to send and receive images***; iii) ***data captured by each camera/microphone is transmitted to the other people via the network***; iv) ***each user views and hears the other participants from their computer***.

Award 1 mark for each of two correct points.

(c) (ii) Benefits include: i) ***cuts down on travel costs***; ii) ***staff can spend more time at work and less time travelling***; iii) ***teleconferences can be arranged more quickly than face-to-face meetings***; iv) ***it's easier to discuss things in a teleconference than over the phone.***

Award 1 mark for each of two correct benefits.

5 (a) Differences include: i) ***desktop computers are bigger and heavier so they tend to stay in one place, laptops are smaller and lighter and are designed to be portable***; ii) ***desktop computers usually have more memory capacity than laptops***; iii) ***desktop computers can only operate using mains electricity, laptops can operate using battery power***; iv) ***desktop computers usually have bigger screens than laptops***; v) ***desktop computers are usually cheaper to buy than laptops***.

Award 1 mark for each of two correct differences.

To be awarded a mark each answer must compare the two types of equipment. Answers that just describe a feature of one type of computer should be awarded no marks.

(b) Benefits include: i) ***laptops can be used in different classrooms***; ii) ***the number of laptops can be matched to the number of pupils in a class***; iii) ***pupils can take laptops home***; iv) ***the school doesn't need a computer room***; v) ***children can't hide behind their computers as easily.***

Award 1 mark for each of two correct benefits.

(c) Problems include: i) ***more expensive to buy than desktop computers***; ii) ***more likely to get damaged than desktop computers***, iii) ***harder to connect to a network than desktop computers***; iv) ***easier for a laptop to go missing/be stolen than a desktop computer***.

Award 1 mark for each of two correct problems.

6 (a) The fields are: ***Author***; ***Title***; ***Stock number***; ***Date last loaned***; ***Date returned***.

Award 1 mark for one correct field.

(b) Key field is ***Stock number***.

Award 1 mark if correct key field identified.

(c) Answers include: i) ***so that each individual record can be uniquely identified***; ii) ***so that a search can be carried out to identify a particular book***; iii) ***otherwise a particular book could not be specifically identified***.

Award 2 marks for a clear understanding of the key field enabling an individual record in the database to be identified. Award 1 mark if the reference to an individual record or book is missing.

(d) ***When a new book is added to the library collection***.

Award 1 mark for a correct reason.

(e) Answers include: i) ***if a customer borrows a book***; ii) ***if a customer returns a book***; iii) ***if a book's details are found to be incorrect.***

Award 1 mark for a correct reason.

(f) ***If a book is withdrawn from stock or lost.***

Award 1 mark for a correct reason.

7 (a) (i) Answers include: i) ***range check***; ii) ***presence check***; iii) ***check digit***; iv) ***data type check***.

Award 1 mark for each of two correct methods.

(ii) Answers include: i) ***validation can only check whether data is of the right type, not that the data is accurate***; ii) ***for example a range check between 0 and 100 will fail to spot that a percentage of 65 has been incorrectly entered as 56***.

Award 1 mark for one correct point.

(b) Answer is "***No***".

Award 1 mark for correct answer.

(c) Answers include: i) ***to make sure that she typed it correctly the first time***; ii) ***to verify that the data entered the first time is correct***.

Award 2 marks if a correct reference to verification. Award 1 mark for a correct point without a reference to verification.

8 Answers are: booking an airline ticket (***real-time***);
paying the weekly wages (***batch***);
monitoring the temperature inside a nuclear reactor (***real-time***);
calculating gas bills (***batch***).

Award 1 mark for each correct response.

9 (a) Answers include: i) ***a model is a program that represents an object or situation in the real world; a simulation is an activity carried out using the model***; ii) ***a model consists of equations and instructions; a simulation uses those equations and instructions***.

Award 2 marks if answer includes both what a model contains and how it is different to a simulation. Award 1 mark for one correct point.

(b) Benefits include: i) ***can be cheaper than using a real plane***; ii) ***can simulate landing at a number of different airports***; iii) ***can simulate flying in different weather conditions***; iv) ***less dangerous than flying a real plane***; v) ***can simulate conditions/situations/emergencies that would be impractical or too dangerous to practise in a real plane.***

Award 1 mark for each of two correct benefits.

(c) Answers include: i) ***might not be as realistic as the real thing***; ii) ***errors in the programming or inaccurate data may make the simulation different to the real thing***; iii) ***realistic simulators can be very expensive***.

Award 1 mark for one correct point.

10 (a) Answers include: i) ***information is data that has meaning to the user***; ii) ***data is information without meaning or context***; iii) ***data is the name for the information which is put onto a computer system***.

Award 2 marks for an answer that shows a clear understanding of the data/context issue. Award 1 mark for a partial understanding.

(b) Content of the form can include: ***name***; ***address***; ***telephone number***; ***e-mail address***; ***date of birth***; ***previous dentist***.

Award 2 marks for four or more items of data, award 1 mark for two or three items of data. Award 1 mark extra for a well-designed form.

(c) Benefits include: i) ***documents take up less storage space than using a paper-based system of filing cabinets***; ii) ***it is quicker to locate a specific piece of information***; iii) ***information on each patient can be edited more quickly than using a paper-based system***; iv) ***reports can be produced more quickly than using a paper-based system***; v) ***it is easier to search the database***.

Award 1 mark for each of three correct benefits.

11 (a) Answers include: i) ***enables software to communicate with hardware***; ii) ***to run applications software such as a word processor***; iii) ***to manage the system's resources, for example operating two pieces of software at the same time***; iv) ***monitors the system and gives prompts to the user***.

Award 1 mark for each of three correct points.

(b) Answers include: i) ***multitasking enables two or more pieces of software to operate at the same time***; ii) ***the operating system divides processing time between the various pieces of software (time slices) so that it appears to the user that two or more things are happening at the same time***.

Award 1 mark for each of two correct points.

12 Improvements include: i) ***better positioning of the text, for example centre alignment***; ii) ***use of different formatting (size, bold etc.) to emphasise parts of the text***; iii) ***more relevant graphics, for example computers and/or pupils***; iv) ***more information, for example where the club takes place***.

Award 1 mark for each of three improvements. Different text-formatting improvements (style, size, bold, underline etc.) count as 1 mark.

13 (a) Answers include: i) ***bank sort code***; ii) ***bank account number***; iii) ***cheque number***.

Award 1 mark for each of two correct points.

(b) Benefits include: i) ***faster processing of cheques***; ii) ***less chance of error***; iii) ***fewer staff needed to process cheques***, iv) ***harder for criminals to make counterfeit cheques***.

Award 1 mark for each of two correct benefits.

(c) Answer is ***optical character recognition***.

Award 1 mark for correct answer.

(d) (i) Answer is: ***quick to locate a specific item of data because the computer knows exactly where each field starts and finishes***.

Award 1 mark for correct answer.

(ii) Answers include: i) ***each item of data takes up the same amount of memory, so the database can require a lot of memory***; ii) ***it can't store data properly that's longer than the fixed field length (e.g. a surname longer than 25 characters)***.

Award 1 mark for each of two correct answers.

14 Benefits include: i) ***greater access to information***; ii) ***ability to shop from home***; iii) ***ability to bank/pay bills etc. from home***; iv) ***greater ability to work from home***; v) ***able to communicate with a wider group of people via e-mail, internet chat rooms and newsgroups***; vi) ***businesses able to sell their products worldwide***; vii) ***enables people to communicate with people with different cultural backgrounds.***

Problems include: i) ***easier for people to access material such as pornography***; ii) ***less face-to-face contact as people spend more time communicating via the internet***; iii) ***people without access to the technology are excluded from the benefits***; iv) ***small businesses can suffer***; v) ***makes certain crimes easier (including organised crime)***; vi) ***may help to increase the pace of life/accelerate globalisation***; vii) ***people can become 'addicted' to the internet (it can take over people's lives).***

Award 1 mark for each of six sensible and relevant points. Award a maximum of four points if only the benefits or problems are discussed.

GCSE ICT Higher Tier Paper 3B

Section A multiple choice answers

1	C
2	B
3	A
4	C
5	B
6	B
7	D
8	C
9	C
10	C
11	D
12	A

Section B

13 (a) Answers include: i) ***place a suitable sensor in the river***; ii) ***choose a suitable logging interval and logging period***; iii) ***connect the sensor to a computer***; iv) or ***store the readings inside the computer***; v) or ***transmit the readings via radio signal***; vi) ***save the readings for later analysis***.

Award 1 mark for each of four correct points.

(b) (i) Answers include: i) ***system to compare readings with preset value***; ii) ***if readings fall below limit an output signal is sent to a telephone transmitter***; iii) ***the transmitter will send a preset message to Robin's mobile phone***.

Award 1 mark for each of two correct points.

(ii) One possible system is shown below:

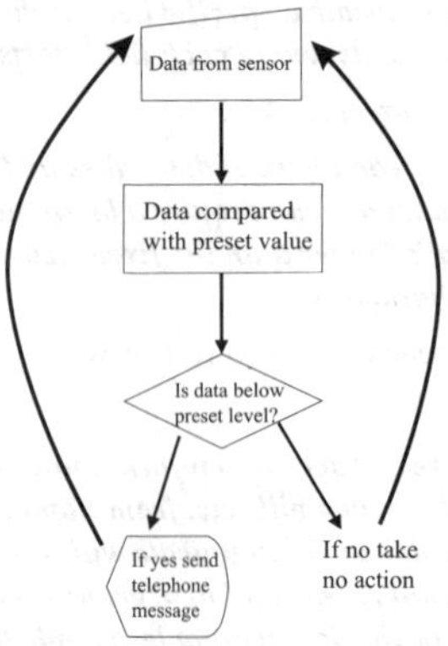

Award 1 mark for each correct part of the diagram, to a maximum of 4 marks.

(c) Answers include: i) ***he could use dummy data***; ii) ***for example he could use data that he knows lies below the preset level***; iii) ***or he could place the sensor in water that he knew to be sufficiently deoxygenated***; iv) ***he could then see if the system sent a message***; v) ***he could then repeat this with data above the preset level; this time the message should not be sent***.

Award 1 mark for each of four correct points.

14 (a) Answer includes: i) ***the DTP software is used to combine information produced in other programs***; ii) ***text and tables can be produced using a word processor***; iii) ***graphs of data are produced using a spreadsheet and graphing software***; iv) ***images can be taken from a clip art library; digital photographs or prints which have been scanned can be manipulated using photo-editing software***; v) ***the DTP program can be used to improve the layout of the newspaper***; vi) ***a computer file containing the newspaper can then be sent to the printers***.

Award 1 mark for each of five correct points.

(b) Benefits include: i) ***changes to the newspaper can be made right up until the printing deadline***; ii) ***journalists can input their stories directly onto the newspaper***; iii) ***digital photographs (or scanned photos) can be edited to improve their appearance***; iv) ***the newspaper can be produced more quickly***; v) ***this can save money***; vi) ***easier to change layout***; vii) ***can perform spell checks etc.***; viii) ***can use facilities like full justification to improve the layout***.

Award 2 marks for each benefit if the benefits to the publishers have been made clear. Otherwise award 1 mark for each of two benefits identified.

(c) Implications include: i) ***staff may suffer from health problems such as eye strain, headaches and repetitive-strain injury (RSI)***; ii) ***staff may need to take regular breaks away from their computers***; iii) ***staff may be entitled to free eye tests***; iv) ***the publisher will need to provide a healthy working environment, for example by providing proper chairs and good lighting***; v) ***the publisher will need to ensure all electrical equipment and cables are in a safe condition***; vi) ***all staff will need to take reasonable precautions to ensure the safety of themselves and others***.

Award 1 mark for each of four correct points.

(d) Reasons include: i) ***the file might have been corrupted***; ii) ***the file might contain a virus***; iii) ***the file might be of a type that is not recognised by the publisher's computer system***; iv) ***the file could be password-protected***.

Award 1 mark for each of two correct points.

(e) (i) Answers include: i) ***the search engine scans the relevant pages and stores information about them in its database***; ii) ***the user searches for specific information by giving the search engine one or more keywords***; iii) ***the search engine matches the keyword(s) to the data in its database***; iv) ***information about the pages that matches the search criteria is displayed to the user***; v) ***the list is usually sorted by the relevance of the pages or the number of times that the keyword(s) appear(s) in each page***.

Award 1 mark for each of three correct points.

(ii) Reasons can include: i) ***to reduce the amount of memory needed to store the web site***; ii) ***because they have evidence that people do not wish to view stories older than six months***; iii) ***to reduce the time it takes to search for particular news stories***; iv) ***to reduce the financial cost of operating the web site***; v) ***because information in the older stories is more likely to be out of date***.

Award 1 mark for each of two correct reasons.

(f) (i) Answers include: i) ***to reach a greater number/wider range of people***; ii) ***to try to sell more products***; iii) ***to enable them to carry out market research***; iv) ***can be cheaper than advertising in print***; v) ***adverts can be interactive (e.g. they can include a link to the company's web site)***.

Award 1 mark for each of three relevant points.

(ii) Answers include: i) ***because they are worried that people could take unauthorised copies of the logo***; ii) ***they are worried that unauthorised copies of the logo could be changed and reposted onto the internet***.

Award 1 mark for each of two correct points.

15 Relevant points include:

Features of computer-aided learning:

i) ***use of interactive learning tools on CD-ROM***;

ii) ***use of the internet to generate and share ideas***;

iii) ***use of computer-based testing with instant feedback***.

Benefits of this trend:

i) ***pupils should be more motivated***;

ii) ***pupils can get instant feedback on progress***;

iii) ***pupils have access to a wider range of learning resources***;

iv) ***pupils can exchange work more easily between school and home***;

v) ***pupils' skills and confidence in using ICT will improve***;

vi) ***pupils are gaining valuable life skills***.

Problems with this trend:

i) ***the equipment is expensive to install, maintain and upgrade***;

ii) ***some schools lack the money to invest in lots of up-to-date ICT equipment***;

iii) ***teachers may need extra training***;

iv) ***may reduce ability in other areas, e.g. ability and motivation to read printed texts***;

v) ***may help to reduce concentration span***;

vi) ***pupils may be able to gain access to inappropriate material from the internet (e.g. pornography)***;

vii) ***pupils without access to ICT at home may be at a disadvantage***.

Award 1 mark for each of nine relevant points.